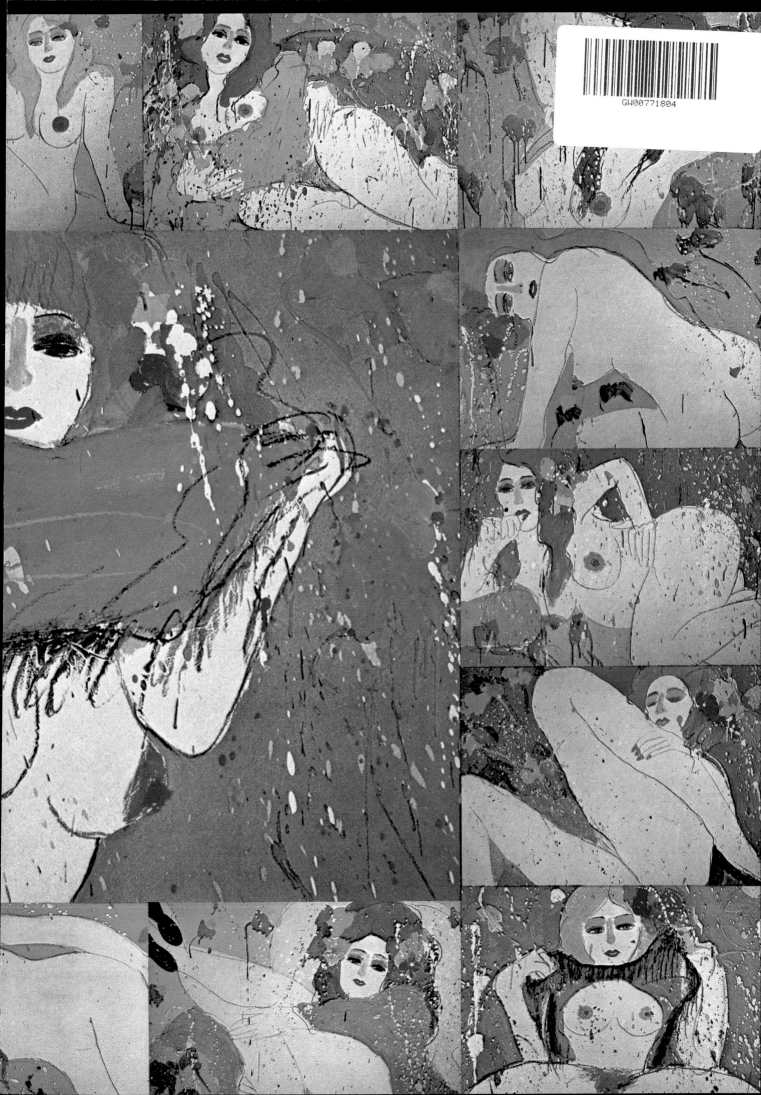

Twentieth Century

MASTERS OF EROTIC ART

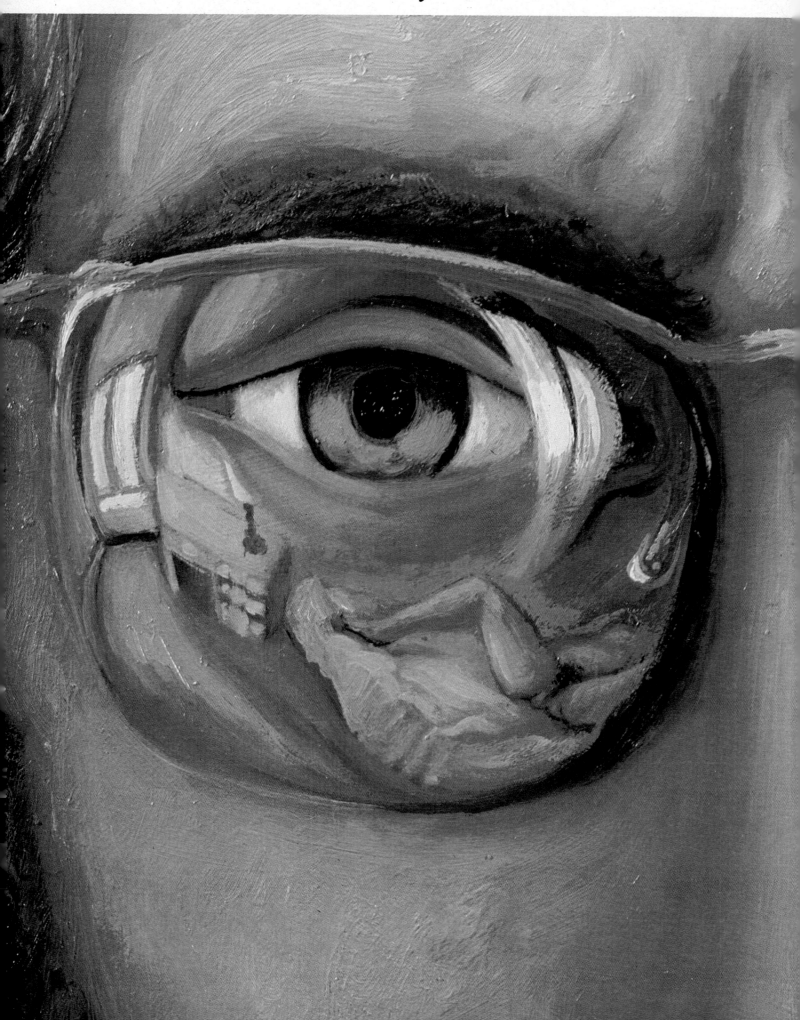

EROTIC ART

BRADLEY SMITH
Fleetbooks Inc. New York

Front jacket

JEAN PAUL CLEREN *one of Europe's most popular artists has created this scene of romantic love with the building blocks of life. Cleren lives and works in France.*

Back jacket

RYONOSUKE FUKUI *a Japanese artist has been exhibited all over the world. This work is from his monograph* Sei To Shi No Tame No Shusaku *(Study for Life and Death) published by Tokyo's Fujii Gallery. Title:* Ai *(Love).*

Frontispiece

JOSÉ PUIGMARTI VALLES *the Spanish artist has painted this sensational* Portrait of Sylvia Bourdon *in 1979. It combines her female beauty with erect male symbols to create both a male and a female fantasy.*

Title page

ANTHONY GREEN *the British artist takes a split vision look at a middle-aged erotic couple in a striking detail from this recent painting entitled* Chelsea Checker. *A member of the prestigious Royal Academy, Green paints in London.*

Half title page

BERNARD LOUEDIN *the French artist who lives on the coast of Brittany has used shapes from sea shells and coastal rocks as a setting for the eternal embrace. A man and a woman are gracefully joined in this romantic painting that he has entitled:* Sève d'Automne *(Juice of Autumn).*

End papers

WALASSE TING *the New York artist painted these sensuous women. They are reproduced from the limited edition of* Red Mouth, *an extraordinary book of his art and poetry.*

A Gemini Smith, Inc. Book

Conceived, written and produced by Bradley Smith

Consultant: Dr. J.-M. Lo Duca

Designer: Mary Johnson

Text Editor: Booton Herndon

Coordinator: Elisabeth Girard Smith

Permissions: S.P.A.D.E.M., Paris, V.A.G.A., A.D.A.G.P., New York;
Copyright © 1980 by Bradley Smith
Library of Congress Catalog Card Number: 80-36666

Published by:
Fleetbooks
c/o Feffer and Simons Inc.
100 Park Avenue
New York, N.Y. 10016

International Standard Book Number 0-517-542366

Printed in Italy

TABLE OF CONTENTS

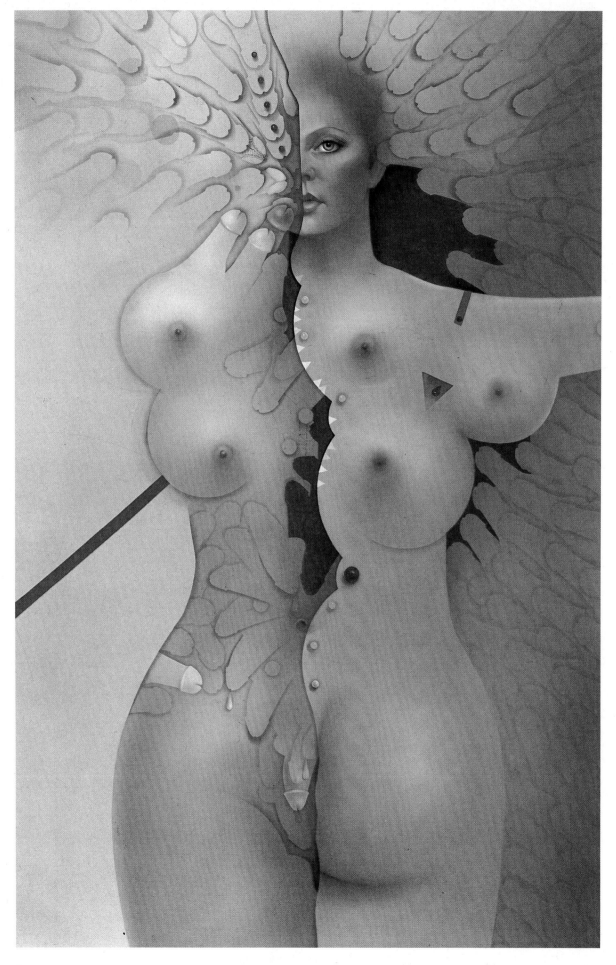

6

PREFACE

There is nothing abstract about erotic art. The artist is out to define male and female sexuality; the subjects are recognizable. The surface scene may be as thin as new ice, but down below, the sexual fires burn brilliantly. The viewer may wonder what the artist means but he never has to ask what the painting is about.

By viewing the erotic paintings of contemporary artists we can hope to understand some of our sexual frustrations as well as our satisfactions. We may even make some astonishing discoveries about how we feel about sex. In an age when we are desperately seeking enlightenment about our own sexuality, the insight of twentieth century artists can help us explore our own potential. This is not to say that erotic art will cure our sexual anxiety, but it adds to our knowledge and helps us as humans to see deeper into ourselves.

As twentieth century society began to examine its sexual impulses and individuals to accept responsibity for their own emotions, the artists among us gained the freedom to examine our unspoken sexual urges and explore more fully the highs and lows of human desire. Out of these explorations came a knowledge of the importance of fantasy, humor, symbols, and romance in art. This is a new concept—for such understanding was unknown as recently as the nineteenth century.

Yet the artist has always occupied a very special place. In the past thirty years he has been allowed to shake our everyday beliefs about sex and its mysteries, to offer ideas that ordinary mortals cannot or do not express. He has made it possible for us to communicate with one another through his images. As the artist grows he knows more of what he knows.

His earlier work (and the work of artists before him) serves as a base for further erotic adventures of the mind.

We live in a society where sex is widely and wildly exploited. Television, motion pictures, newspapers, plays, all devote much time and space to erotic themes. The important difference between sex exploitation and erotic art lies in the sensitivity and talent of the artist. If the imagination and technique of the artist is permanently stamped on the work, the artist has successfully translated his emotions and observations into visual meanings. A miniature world has been created within each painting. Within this world, strong feelings become images and at some point the work takes on its own individuality—its own meaning. This meaning may be difficult to read. At times he may be able to use traditional visual language and symbols, or he may invent a new visual language.

Artists of earlier generations who painted direct allusions to the sexual life of humans painted for themselves and a very limited audience of friends and patrons. The painter's reputation and all of his future earnings could be jeopardized by the censorship of critics, art dealers who controlled galleries and, especially, repressive governments. He could be, and often was, cast out of polite society.

The twentieth century changed all that. As artists were allowed to paint openly, to reveal private dreams, fantasies, romances, and even realism, the basis changed. The artist began an exploration of the multiple channels of sexual creativity which are as endless as the process of procreation itself.

Twentieth century artists, themselves searchers into self knowledge, have increasingly revealed not only their own view of sex, but insight into universal sexuality. Today the pleasurable act of sexual contact can be visualized, and the capacity for pleasure and pain in sex can be more clearly and more poetically defined. No longer is it necessary for sexually intimate scenes to be confined to heterosexuals. Artists and scientists have understood that humans are a precariously balanced combination of male and female qualities and preferences; and that male, female, and homo-sexuality all exist in varying degrees.

The hope expressed in 1538 by the Roman poet Aretino has come true. He wrote: *"What harm is there in seeing a man on top of a woman? Must the animals have more freedom than we? It seems to me that the you-know-what given us by nature for the preservation of the species should be worn as a pendent around our necks or a badge in our caps...it has produced the pretty children and the beautiful women with their sancta sanctorum and for this reason we should decree holy days and dedicate vigils and feasts in its honor not hide it away in scraps of cloth and silk."*

At one time or another, most great painters have created specifically erotic works which were not available for public viewing. In the eighteenth and nineteenth centuries among the artists were Courbet, Fragonard, Watteau, Boucher, Rowlandson, Turner, Daumier, Degas, Millet, and many, many others. Their erotic paintings which had been kept out of sight so many years are now being widely displayed in art galleries, museums, libraries and the bookstores. Some of the paintings first reproduced in my previous volume, *Erotic Art of the Masters,* are now in major museums. Notably, Sir Stanley Spencer's *The Leg of Mutton,* which shows the artist and his wife nude beside a glowing stove and a raw leg of mutton, is now prominently displayed in London's Tate Gallery. A series of Edgar Degas etchings illustrating *Madame Tellier's Brothel* by Guy de Maupassant was shown at the Louvre in 1979. Major exhibitions of erotic art have been held by the Sidney Janis Gallery, the Alex Rosenberg Gallery and the New School for Social Research Gallery in New York, and by the Beaubourg Museum in Paris. Major museum exhibits have been held in London, Paris, Brussels, and Berlin.

As with all art, erotic painting is a quest. In this search the strange, bizarre or fantastic becomes understandable. In erotic paintings the essence of the sex drive is brought to visual realization. Such paintings are sexually stimulating. They may pique the curiosity of the viewer, reveal a new view of sensuality, they may even have a direct physical effect on the viewer.

Since 1960, themes in erotic paintings have dealt with the fast changing sexual customs of western society. Women no longer are shown as sex objects but as full participants in all kinds of sexual activities. Indeed a considerable number of erotic paintings are created by women. Among those represented in this book are Clara Tice, Leonor Fini, Jo Manning Heard, Martha Edelheit, and Mary Frank.

In this book dealing with the twentieth century masters, I have arbitrarily decided upon certain categories under which the paintings are displayed. These categories do not reflect specific "schools" of painting, nor do they refer to previous schools such as the Romantic or Symbolist schools of the eighteenth century. What I have done is to use descriptive

9

words such as Romance, Fantasy, Beyond Realism, and others as a convenient way of dividing the book into chapters. In many cases readers, critics, and the artists themselves will argue that certain paintings should not be placed in one category or another. In many instances they will be right. But it has seemed to me that some of the paintings fall into the area of romance. And by romance, I mean exactly that: they reflect a romantic feeling toward sex. Others fall into the realm of sexual fantasy. And while fantasy is very close to symbolism, they are not quite interchangeable. I have elected to call one chapter "The Erotic Smile" because it seems to me that in this chapter an all-pervading sense of joy and laughter, of satire and cynicism are appropriately combined.

Some of the artists' greatest works may not be included here for the reason that this is a very personal collection. It is subjective; it represents what I think were their most interesting erotic works. It does not and could not include all the important artists who have painted erotica.

I have included five short essays as parts of the overall erotic mosaic in order to give some sense of the evolution of erotica from the beginning to the present. These essays are devoted to the innovators, the builders of modern erotic work. They include Pablo Picasso, Salvador Dali, and Hans Bellmer, and writers, D.H. Lawrence and Henry Miller, who were also painters and whose influence has been profound.

There is no chronological grouping of pictures. Some artists painting before 1920 are as modern in their approach to contemporary eroticism as those painters whose works were created in 1980.

Finally, the painting of erotic pictures, of sensuous images, has nothing to do with sexual morality. Sex, in art, has a value of its own. Sex, in life, has a value of its own. Sexual ethics or morals are not in conflict with erotic painting. The artist does not recommend a sexual distinction, a sexual direction or his preference to the viewer. He looks inside himself, observes his environment, and creates a work of art out of it.

The incredibly creative artist of the early twentieth century, Marcel Duchamp, once said, "the great artists of tomorrow will go underground." We can be grateful that he was dead wrong. The great innovative artists of the twentieth century have never been so popular or so widely exhibited.

Bradley Smith
La Jolla, California

Reflections on Erotica
by Henry Miller

Over the years, beginning in 1967, I have enjoyed long and stimulating conversations with my friend Henry Miller. Our subjects ranged over literature, sex, and art. Fortunately, I had my tape recorder turned on as we talked. Here are some of Henry's observations as I recorded them.

...It is the thought of sex that is interesting to me, everything connected with the realm of sex intrigues me.

...I was talking one day to some Japanese girls. They said they were disgusted with "porno" films. Sheer dirt. I don't agree. I say it's unnatural for anyone to turn his eyes away no matter how lousy the films are. It's a cock and a cunt and they are fucking and it's exciting. Erotic literature and art after all is such an elemental force. Fucking is more than sex. It's just as magical and mysterious as talking about God or the nature of the Universe.

...One wonders sometimes what is the ideal setting for love making, the most inspiring ambiance for making love. Is it the bedroom, with plush rose-colored walls and mirrors everywhere? Or is it the icy igloo, soundproof, weatherproof, isolated from the world, in which the lovers lie naked and warm between thick bearskin? Or is it the parked car in a vacant lot with the radio turned on full blast? Could it be that with all the artistry and skill, all the aesthetic surroundings that civilized man has introduced to render this simple act more enjoyable, he has lost what any mongrels in the street enjoy when helplessly coupled, one pulling north and the other south, as they wait patiently for someone in the crowd to throw a pail of cold water over them?

...Straight pictures, photographs that is, of cunts and pricks and people fucking may be stimulating but the work of a truly great erotic painter hits harder and its influence may last for hundreds of years.

...That's the definition in my mind of an artist, that he is only a man who rearranges things. Arthur Rimbaud said, "no man ever created anything." Man is not a creator. All man does is turn things about, rearrange things, that's all. That's creation as far as man goes.

...There are no new ways of sex, only different ways of portraying it. As a man rearranges his life style his sexual ways change with it. We get the kind of art that reflects these changes. We get what we deserve...and the wonder of it is that our civilization allows us the freedom to view the world as it is.

...I'm always glad to see a painting by George Grosz for the more I see of his work the more I wonder at his use of color. He was a master. In his early paintings sex was the thing and even though his subject and treatment were brutal and even horrible it is an aesthetic treat for all of us. The first painting I ever made was a copy of a painting by Grosz.

...What can I say about art? Well, nothing matters to me so long as it works. I believe in letting the magic of creation take over. The question about a painting should not be "is it true?" or "is it likely to last?"...but, "does it work? Is it what the artist wanted it to be?"

...Ezra Pound once wrote, "no art ever yet grew by looking into the eyes of the public."

...When I look back at myself there is no one self to recall. The different kinds of self surprise me. The things that stimulated me at one time have no effect at another. I think all artists, I'm speaking of painters, are always looking for something—something that will explain some aspect of the world to them. In erotic art the painter searches for a meaning in sex. He may not find it but the search itself is meaningful and gives satisfaction and meaning to his life.

...Age has much to do with the effect of erotic pictures or erotic literature— the works of Casanova, Rabelais or Boccacio, which may have got my juices running as a young man, would not have that effect today. The same is somewhat true of erotic paintings yet there is a difference because I've always been a bit of a voyeur. Painting interests me, has always interested me, very much. But like erotic literature, it has no effect unless it is done by an artist.

Henry Miller portrayed himself in this merry watercolor which includes a number of erotic symbols.

13

THE EROTIC SMILE

In spite of the Latin saying *post coitum tristis* (after fucking, sadness), humor and sex have made a merry mixture. It's the absence of sex that makes for sadness as most men and women readily admit.

Perhaps the oldest verse involving an erotic artist points out the preference for sex over painting:

While Titian was mixing rose madder
His model posed nude on a ladder
Her position, to Titian
Suggested coition
So he climbed up the ladder and had 'er.

Twentieth century artists have happily painted this lighter side of sex. Revealing scenes abstracted from life affirm that sex need not always be serious. In the pages that follow, the viewers will find ocular double entendre, excesses, exaggerations, slapstick comedy, satire and the element of surprise. One may find oneself being a voyeur to yet another voyeur, as if seeing oneself in a distorted triple mirror at a carnival sideshow. There is no repression in these paintings, no rules of subject matter;

there is only the insight and smile of the artist.

Authors and poets led the way to this humorous attitude toward human sexuality. They had precedents in the nineteenth century. One of them, the great landscape artist, J.M.W. Turner, painted a number of highly charged erotic watercolors. During his lifetime he was careful to allow only his friends to see them, and after his death they were secreted in the files of the British Museum. There, the famous but sexually up-tight British art critic, John Ruskin, discovered them. Horrified that a famous British artist had painted "dirty pictures," he burned them, with the approval of the Trustees of the Museum. That these lost erotic visions were amusing as well as revealing is indicated by a Turner verse preserved for us uncensored:

"The critical moment no maid can withstand,
when a bird in the bush is worth two in the hand."

Writers in earlier centuries—Shakespeare, Voltaire, Rabelais, Robert Burns—all had revealed their knowledge of the erotic smile. Often the erotic laugh occurs in their accounts of the human comedy. Twentieth century writers continued to see the amusing aspects of sex. Even William Faulkner (who was never known for humor) wrote in *Sanctuary*:

"Yes Sir," Minnie said, "the two of them would be nekkid as two snakes, and Popeye hanging over the foot of the bed without even his hat on making a kind of a whinnying sound." "Maybe he was cheering for them," Miss Lorraine said, "the lousy son of a bitch."

Other writers of the late twentieth century could and did record the sexual smile. In Vladimir Nabokov's *Lolita*, what could be more visually hilarious than the scene in which Humbert has carefully planned to seduce his stolen nymphet:

Her kiss, to my delirious embarassment, had some rather comical refinements of flutter and probe which made me conclude she had been coached at an early age by a little Lesbian. No Charlie boy could have taught her that. As if to see

Does an old man recall an erotic encounter of his youth, or does he fantasize a liaison that has never happened? With a sense of satire that combines humor and nostalgia, the artist R.B. Kitaj opens the mind's door to a congeries of erotic memories.

15

whether I had my fill and learned the lesson, she drew away and surveyed me. Her cheekbones were flushed, her full underlip glistened, my dissolution was near. All at once, with a burst of rough glee (the sign of the nymphet!), she put her mouth to my ear—but for quite a while my mind could not separate into words the hot thunder of her whisper, and she laughed, and brushed the hair off her face, and tried again, and gradually the odd sense of living in a brand new, mad new dream world, where everything was permissible, came over me as I realized what she was suggesting. I answered I did not know what game she and Charlie had played. "You mean you have never—?"—her features twisted into the stare of disgusted incredulity. "You have never—" she started again. I took time out by nuzzling her a little. "Lay off, will you," she said with a twangy whine, hastily removing her brown shoulder from my lips. (It was very curious the way she considered—and kept doing so for a long time—all caresses except kisses on the mouth or the stark act of love either "romantic slosh" or "abnormal.")

"You mean," she persisted, now kneeling above me, "you never did it when you were a kid?"

"Never," I answered quite truthfully.

"Okay," said Lolita, "here is where we start."

Andy Warhol, in *Blue Movie*, included conversation while his two characters were fucking:

Viva: I wish you'd get harder.
Louis: Harder than what?
Viva: Harder than you are.
Louis: In the Greek Theatre when the guys came out with hard-ons everybody used to laugh.
Viva laughs!

But sexual humor was rarely if ever seen in the paintings of fine artists until the 1960s. Then there was the work of Aubrey Beardsley, full of satiric touches and barely concealed sex symbols. But the most erotic drawings of Beardsley were surpressed, as were those of Félicien Rops and Jules Pascin.

With the 60's the erotic smile and the human side of sexuality began to be publicly displayed. Erotic paintings by Tom Wesselmann, Kitaj, Larry Rivers, Paul Wunderlich, and little known early works by André Masson and George Grosz were shown by the most respectable art galleries in the world. The Sidney Janis Gallery had a major showing of erotic paintings and sculpture in 1966 and then there was no stopping the demand for good erotic paintings. Others such as the Louise Leiris Gallery in Paris, the Marlborough Gallery in New York, and the Gallery of the New School for Social Research followed. Artists showed works that reflected and explained human emotion in terms of human sexuality. Men and women and their various sexual relationships were examined from the inside out. Not only were the sexual mores of the twentieth century revealed by the new generation of painters, but the earlier nineteenth and twentieth century erotic artists were shown. Their works increased both in exposure and price. The kind of freedom to see sex in the context of the human comedy, earlier accorded writers, now passed to artists.

The erotic smile sometimes depends upon understatement, on allusion—sometimes illusion, for the arousal of the sexual instinct. A flower seen as a vulva, breasts seen as mountains, a penis as the Eiffel Tower or the Empire State Building, add imagination and more than one meaning to the work. This is more than symbolism. It is humanity taking an amused look at itself. Such graphic sexual allusions can be deeply revealing of human behavior. Satiric comments made when the mind of the artist extends to his hand and canvas often present a more shocking revelation than a page of written text.

The shared experience of artists who live and paint in our society offers an understanding of the gaiety, joy and laughter of modern sex life in all its forms and colors.

In Pablo Picasso's large exhibition in 1966-67 many works dealt with the erotic theme. Surprisingly, it opened at the Palais des Papes (Pope's Palace) in Avignon. It then moved to the Louise Leiris Gallery in Paris. Although the painter was eighty-five years old his work was original, imaginative, and vigorous. He viewed sexuality with a smile.

It must be mentioned here that the artists whose work is reproduced in this chapter do not always perceive eroticism as humorous. Other of their works may depict tragedy, violence, despair, anger. But on the stimulating pages that follow one sees a broad selection of important twentieth century paintings which reveal human sexuality as amusing, droll, capricious, beguiling, laughable, and sometimes ridiculous. The artist's erotic smile is clearly visible.

Behind a door that opens outward the artist is both the viewer and the viewed. In this mixed media portrait by Robert Morris the element of surprise is like unexpectedly having a bathroom door burst open. The black and white image is a pleasant shock.

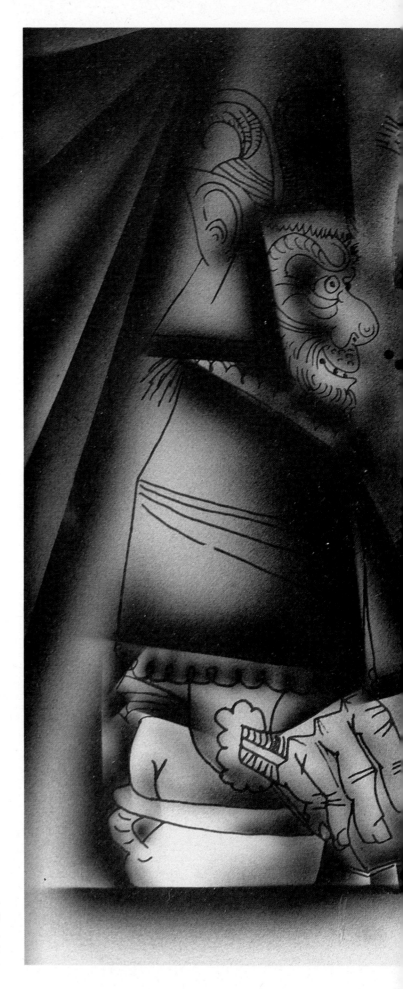

A master of satire, Modesto Roldán painted this hilarious reflection of all the energetic, athletic and erotic line drawings of Picasso. With a probing pen and brush, Roldan has recreated the erotic spirit of the Old King series that was painted by Pablo Picasso in 1964.

18

Roldán et pin...

19

PICASSO EROTICA

It is inevitable that in the years to come many erotic works by Picasso, unknown today, will surface. Intimate sketches of mistresses, wives and friends, tucked away, lost, or hidden; drawings, watercolors and oils—all will emerge as they become increasingly valuable. An example of this type of intimate view is the watercolor of his friend Isidro Nonell (opposite). Others include the De-Soto brothers, sketched in bed with a whore between them, or the Catalan painter Joan Ossó caught in an embarrassing moment with his pants down. These are only a few of the erotic drawings owned by the Museo Picasso in Barcelona, and these works of youthful exuberance, drawn and painted when the artist was between nineteen and twenty-five, in turn represent only a few of the total number known to exist, for in the following seventy years endless works, many erotic, flowed from the brain and hand of this visual giant.

Picasso's erotic works are for the most part cool and humorous rather than hot and passionate. Could it be that because the intense sexual drive of this Spanish painter was so continuously gratified, he was spared the frustration that makes for passion in erotic art?

One cannot help but be envious of this talented, energy-charged, physically powerful and sexually appealing young man, who instead of fantasizing unavailable young women, found them, fucked them, and often painted them. His early life had much in common with his fellow painter Toulouse Lautrec who died when Picasso was twenty. Picasso was impressed by the quality of Lautrec's compassionate paintings of the whores and madames and the high life of the cafes.

Picasso was born a precocious genius. True, he took some lessons, but one gets the impression that he instinctively knew more about painting than the teachers. He understood how to select and absorb appropriate elements of his environment, and was able unthinkingly to translate them into permanent images imbued with the spirit and temper of each passing decade. Surely his intense sexuality contributed to this understanding.

Three periods mark peak performances in Picasso's erotic works. We don't know when his sex life

began, for he had his own studio at the age of sixteen and sold three paintings in Paris at nineteen. But the erotic paintings reproduced here were done when he was twenty or so, prowling the cafes and cathouses of the Barcelona waterfront.

Twenty-four years later, now a recognized master, he turned again to the art of love in 1946-47. This was a time of great happiness in his life. He and Françoise Gilot were at Golfe Juan near Antibes; during this period his son Claude was born. He painted carefree women, men, children, goats, and horses on the beach, all of them naked and unashamed. Real and imaginary creatures cavorted, slim Pan-like creatures with plump pricks and dual flutes played music, centaurs with bulging testicles and sharp-pointed phalluses chased full-breasted girls—and often caught up with them. Simple sexual pleasure in all its phases has rarely been more joyously imagined and artistically recorded than in the Antibes drawings. If Picasso had never made any other drawings, these were enough to have brought him lasting fame.

Six years later came another burst of Picasso's erotic energies. In the canvases of 1954-55 naked models pose for an elderly painter, high-breasted women converse with dwarfs, cupids, and clowns. In one symbolic scene a nude young girl holds a cat while twelve men crowd around her, and in another a very old man reaches for a young girl's breast.

Picasso gave the world still one more erotic feast when, still vigorous at eighty-seven, he showed at the Louise Leiris gallery in Paris a series of erotic engravings that represented the distillation of a well-spent life. One explicit scene followed another; the artist had reached into his sexual past to paint artists dallying with their models, sex life at the circus, scenes inside a brothel. Many etchings include a very old man, sometimes a king (probably Picasso), observing the sexual variations of cunnilingus and fellatio, as well as gymnastic fucking and intricate orgies.

To those critics who accuse Picasso of being cold, unfeeling, even unhuman, his erotic works, in which his warmth and depth of feeling come through magnificently, are a convincing answer. As Henry Miller once wrote, "He is working away at the joints of creation."

Picasso was only twenty-one or twenty-two years old when he painted this intimate scene of his comrade and fellow painter, Isidro Nonell. Rich in humor, his flowing line indicates the technical ability of the young painter as well as his interest in erotica.

The theme of the voyeur is one of the oldest in erotic painting. Here Kitaj has added other elements. The voyeur is in darkness; he might be anyone—even you. And the scene satirizes the myth of the exaggerated magnitude of the black man's phallus.

The erotic smile is evident in a homey erotic scene by
William Copley. The coffee cup, telephone, and easy
attitude of the girl helping her partner undress give it
a folk-like quality. Opposite, with a few bold strokes,
Copley was able to create a very strong erotic image.

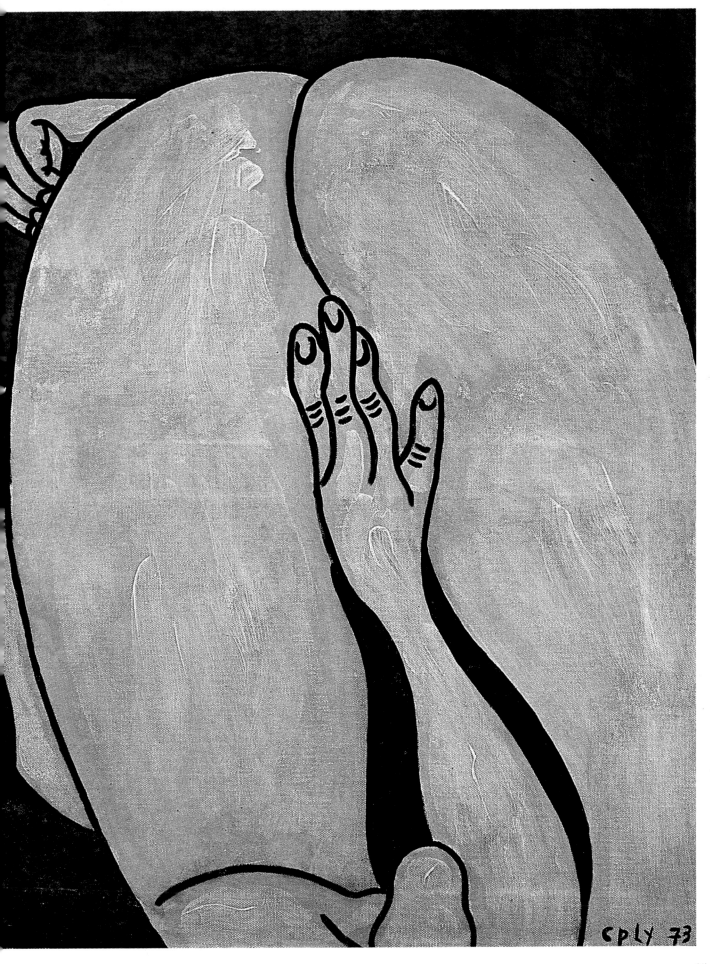

CPLY 73

Alexander Calder, painter, sculptor, and innovator, humorously exploits the abandon o

Calder 67

he human male flaunting his nudity in space. As the master of motion created little erotic art, this is a rarity indeed.

A black whore is being fondled by a sailor in this bizarre concept by the German artist Otto Dix. Some repainting has been done in the lower left-hand corner, possibly in an attempt at censorship. The sailor's hand was doubtless originally placed between the legs of the girl.

HENRY MILLER

More than thirty art exhibits, three to four thousand watercolors, hundreds of sales—does this sound like the author of *Tropic of Cancer*? Is this the same Henry Miller whose literary works were a major force in the gains made in sexual freedom in the twentieth century? It is. Moreover, it is possible that Miller preferred painting to writing and realized more satisfaction from it. He likes to tell of his struggling days in New York, when he sold his watercolors for ten cents, a quarter, or whatever the customer wanted to pay. Landscape, portrait, it made no difference to Miller.

In *To Paint Is To Love Again*, he wrote, "In these miserable expressions of my non-existent talent you will find the flotsam and jetsam (mixed with anchovies and sesame seed), my broken dreams, my imaginary illnesses, my phony ideals." But there were other times when he looked on his watercolors more respectfully.

It was George Grosz who originally got him started. Miller often expressed a great feeling for Grosz. He wrote in *My Life and Times*: "He was a master. His early works were brutal and they were meant to be that: a condemnation of the German nation, the people, the whole people, condemned forever... He left an indelible mark on them."

And on Henry Miller as well, for the first thing Miller did to his own satisfaction was a copy of a Grosz portrait. He then poured out so many watercolors that he staged an exhibition in Greenwich Village. The location was a speakeasy that he and his wife June were operating at the time, but it *was* a first exhibition. For the next half century Henry kept right on painting.

He was largely self-taught, but he knew many artists and sculptors in both New York and Paris, where he lived for the better part of ten years, and he never stopped observing, searching, criticizing. Utrillo, he said, for example, was "boring as hell."

On at least one occasion he put painting before writing. After *Tropic of Cancer,* that earthy classic published in France which, smuggled into England and America by World War II GIs, became a symbol of freedom to write about sex in the English language, Miller was asked to do a book on D.H. Lawrence. Henry admired Lawrence's literary work, but not Lawrence's paintings. "Sometimes when I think of doing a watercolor," he wrote at the time, "I get such a furious hunger and rage that I could destroy the book." He dropped the project.

His own watercolors defy classification. He was influenced by the Surrealists. "Let the brush in the hand dictate," he said. He would start a watercolor wherever he wanted, on a foot, a tree, and then let his brush take its course.

There is eroticism in many of his watercolors, yet Miller never set out to do erotic painting; rather, his work shows innocence and childish exuberance. Even when he took to writing words and phrases for graffiti effect, the so-called four letter words are in German or French.

His erotic paintings always give us something to explore—a naked girl behind a bar, a fat menstruating woman, nudes with vulva and pubic hair crudely displayed. Simplicity and charm make them all inoffensive.

Miller would turn to watercolors when he either could not or would not write. When he fell in love with Hoki Tokuda in 1967, one of the crises in his life, he found it impossible to sleep. Consumed with desire and jealousy, he picked up his brush and turned out the twelve watercolors of the *Insomnia* series, all among the best he has ever painted.

Sometimes I think that Henry Miller would have preferred to have been a painter exclusively. He liked to rise at dawn to peek at a watercolor done the day before. It is, however, a good thing for us all that he did not limit himself to that art form... His sixty years of watercolor painting had no influence on erotic art, but his *writing* freed artists from censorship and gave us all freedom to see their works.

In a rare print the distinguished author Henry Miller sets his imagination free. Although the girl is in the bathroom, her erotic image is outlined on the bedsheet as though her ghost figure remains. Miller freely admitted the influence of contemporary artists.

For Bradley   "d'après Schatz"   Henry Miller 1973

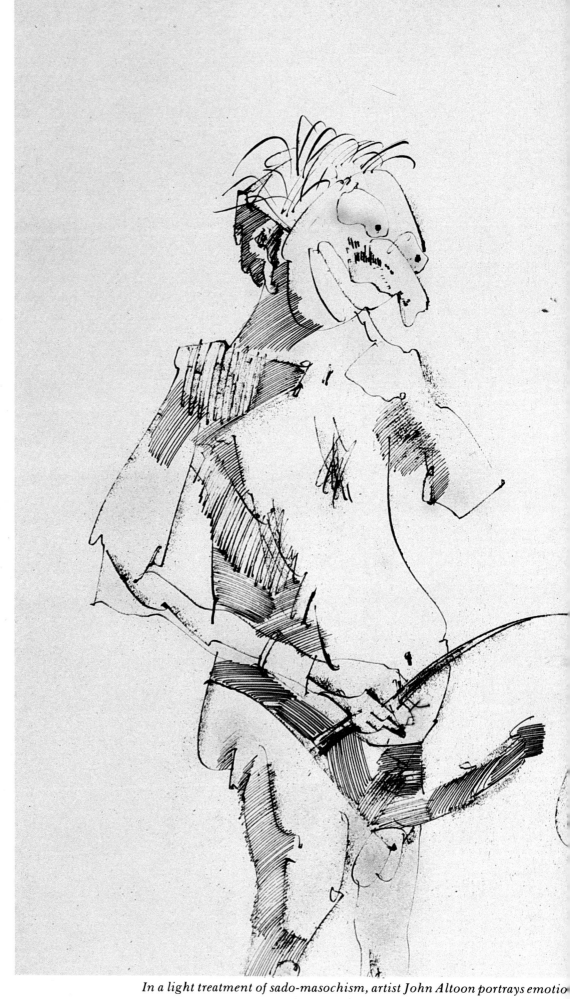

In a light treatment of sado-masochism, artist John Altoon portrays emotio

ftly using only a few lines and subdued color. Note the curve of the whip which calls attention to the demon's huge erection.

In high good humor, New York artist Richard Merkin investigates office sex and erotic business as usual. His Neo-Pop style adds shock value as the apprehensive female views the self-assured boss. Merkin's use of color and space adds to the impact.

(Overleaf) Merkin continues his au courant sexual view in The House of the Two Mysterious Blondes in Their Early Twenties, *in which two naked women caress each other as a "john" awaits his turn. The painting on this page is titled* Charvet et Fils.

34

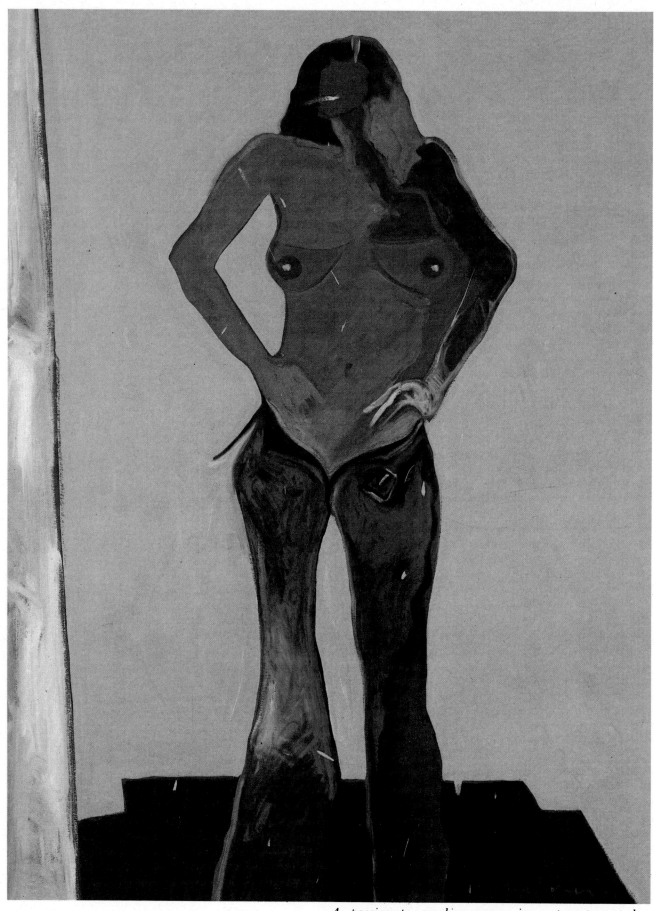

A passionate macho-woman in a transparent bra unzips her jeans in this erotic view by Fritz Scholder, an artist of American Indian-German descent. Using the hot colors of his native Southwest, he has made his model's feminine heat waves more visible.

In Lady Chatterley's Lover, *the erotic novel by D.H. Lawrence, John Thomas was the name gatekeeper Mellors used to address his prick. Walasse Ting, young American-Chinese painter, gives his concept a personality. A title accompanying the portrait reads* Tiger Man.

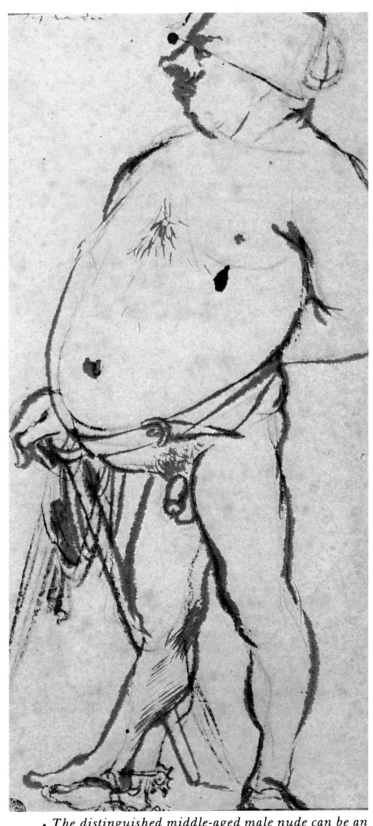

∧ *The distinguished middle-aged male nude can be an erotic figure. Rodin was severely chastised by government and critics when his nude statue of Victor Hugo was unveiled. In this figure drawing Manzù has created a male image in the Rodin tradition.*

< *The consumate satirist of the century, George Grosz seldom held back the irony that flowed from his brush. In this scene an overweight male with an erection pulls his undershirt over his head as his zoftig partner pulls down her panties to await his pleasure.*

42

The English manor house called Stocks is located in the countryside some one hundred miles from London. A contemporary artist, Angela Gorgus was commissioned by its owner Victor Lownes to use it for a series of erotic paintings, that were recently exhibited in England.

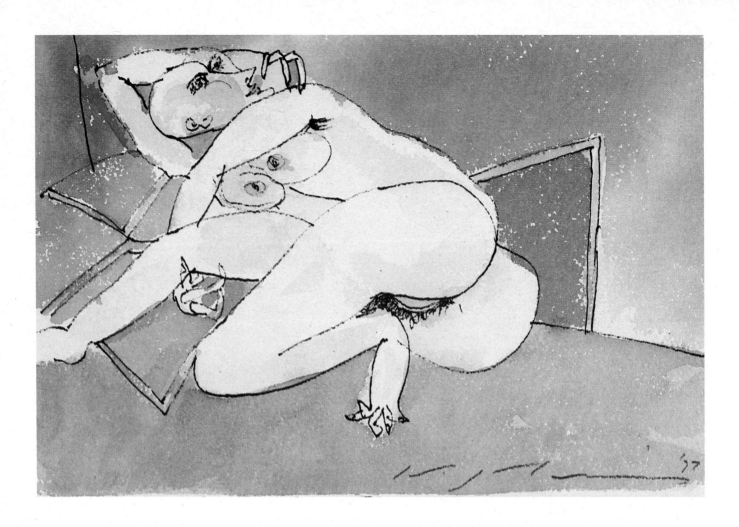

Masuo Ikeda painted these watercolors for an exhibition and reproduced them in a limited edition called **Mixed Fruit**. Ikeda exhibits in New York, Paris and Tokyo. His erotic sketches of women combine lively line technique with highly-charged eroticism.

(Overleaf) Clifton Karhu, Swedish-American, is a master of Japanese scroll and woodblock prints. He is one of Japan's most popular artists and his work is sought after by collectors throughout the world. This erotic scroll has captions in Japanese and English.

In a satiric painting based upon Japanese Shunga the versatile American artist Larry Rivers demonstrates his mastery of line and color. Rivers' style has changed every few years, staying ahead of the cultural scene. Note the woman's toes, curled in orgasm.

FANTASY

Without the ability to fantasize the human mind would be a dull place. For it is in fantasy that the ordinary becomes the special. The copper becomes gold. The unattainable woman or man becomes immediately available.

In the fantasy world of real-unreal the artist can take the viewer for a trip inside his own mind and show the viewer how bizarre, how distinctive, his secret thoughts really are. The viewer, looking at a painting, uses the artist's fantasy as a springboard to take off into explorations of his own. The artist paints a beautiful woman, naked and desirable. For the viewer fantasizing, she is displaying herself for him to enjoy. A woman viewer sees a painting of a narrow-hipped, well-endowed male. In her fantasy he becomes hers and can, in her fantasy, do anything with her she wishes. Everyone fantasizes to a greater or lesser degree. It is easy to enter the world of fantasy with an artist as guide, for in reproducing his fantasy he often reveals our own.

The artist becomes a magician in a strange land where monsters are men and women in disguise. When a dominant male is not available a woman climbs upon and fucks a lion (pages 64-65). In this painting there is a multiple choice of meanings. A male viewer may see himself as the lion, a dominant figure. His fantasy is that a woman has come into his room (cage), stripped off her clothes and mounted him. A female viewer sees a powerful, hairy man. He is passive and he waits for her to enjoy him sexually. She becomes dominant. There is still another element, for the sex act in the open cage may be seen by others, and this may be stimulating. Any form of sexual pleasure may be fantasized with the artist's imaginative guidance; one possibility is cunnilingus with a bear (page 67). We are never fearful of these gentle or even violent monsters, for they are not only part of the artist's mind, they are part of our own.

The world of dreams and the world of fantasies are two quite different places. In an actual dream one may have adventures both pleasant and unpleasant, yet the details are tied to the reality of real objects and of people whose paths have crossed in our conscious hours. But in fantasy, points of reference are conjured up in the conscious rather than the unconscious mind. We may summon them or dismiss them at will. Our fantasies may be pleasant or terrifying, delicate or crude. Their forms are sometimes unbelievably complex, for patterns break into other patterns blending into different forms. Unlike the discipline of Surrealism, painters of fantasy do not break the mold of Classicism. It is sometimes absorbed from other periods. The meaning is changed; the image often distorted. Within the world of fantasy a continuous masquerade goes on. External meanings are easy to read but to find the internal message one must look beneath the exterior for inevitably the apparent meaning wears a disguise.

The freedoms regarding sexual conduct in the twentieth century have brought an awareness of the value of fantasy in eroticism. Masturbation, an important sexual freedom, has ascended from a deadly sin to a pleasant sexual self-to-self response. Yet without the ability to fantasize, it would be almost impossible to successfully masturbate. A number of twentieth century artists, such as Masuo Ikeda (page 45) and Pino Zac (page 73), have effectively explored these masturbatory fantasies and made it possible for many to understand the guiltlessness of this solo pleasure.

The beauty of the female and male genitals has been lovingly recreated in fantasy. That men have long worshipped, even adored, the female breast and vulva has been evidenced by the works of earlier classical as well as avant-garde artists. One can fantasize with these paintings just as one can with the stripteaser, the burlesque queen, or the 10-on-a-scale-of-10 female motion picture star.

In the late twentieth century masculine beauty and strength, which women have long enjoyed observing with downcast eyes, have been recognized and widely represented. The women's magazines, even on the most sophisticated level, have published male nudes. But it is the modern artist, through the use of fantasy, who has continued to

In a never to be forgotten canvas depicting his distinctive world of fantasy, the Paris based artist Ljuba has created a dream figure that is both ugly and beautiful, old and young. Color plays a most important part in this dream image painting.

lead the way in recognition of male beauty. Walasse Ting's surprising *Tiger Man* (page 39), is a truly fantastic expression of the male. The delicate flower garden treatment of the male genitals by Hans Moller (page 102) is vaguely reminiscent of the vulva-like flower paintings by Georgia O'Keeffe.

That the acceptance of the strength and beauty of the male penis has come at last is a tribute to the depth of understanding and the search for beauty by the artist. No longer is this staff of life disguised behind a fig leaf. The glory of man and woman, of pricks and cunts, as D.H. Lawrence would have written, has been recognized in fantasy and reality.

All is by no means peaceful in the fantasy world. Both the artist's fantasies and our own include anxiety, terror, uncertainty and loneliness—as well as sensitivity, need, warmth, desire, tenderness, and love. The key is often in the impression one gets from the artist's creation rather than from its detail.

In fantasy we enter an enchanted place where images are fragmented yet come together to create a new vision. Let us take an example of the use of fantasy by Picasso. In 1905 Picasso was living in Barcelona; his early work was highly erotic. Unwilling to work from second-hand images, the young artist went directly to the whores and the whorehouses of the Carrer d'Avinyo, a back alley on the wild side of the city. In an early sketch for a painting he drew a group of whores sitting and standing around, one squatting with legs open, another pulling her dress over her head, one with one leg crossed, and what seems to be the madam in a dark dress sitting in the center.

But fantasy took over in the actual painting. The women, who in the sketch were somewhat realistically painted, became more angular and the background more spacious. The squatting figure became a possible monster with a face neither male nor female. The painting, finished in 1907, became one of his most famous early efforts, *Les Demoiselles d'Avignon*. In it we see the beginning of Picasso's experiments with Cubist possibilities and the influence of the elongated flat-featured African masks that had become popular in Paris. His creatures are no longer the whores of Barcelona, but characters out of his environment filtered through his imagination.

The great erotic fantasist of the twentieth century is Salvador Dali, who brought images out of fantasy and transformed the idea of space and of time. He painted not only his own world in which everything happened within, but he made a new external world in which space and time were suspended. When a woman fellates a man in this new world, the sexual act is suspended in the space and timelessness that Dali has created (page 187). We find, in Dali's fantasies reaching out from his unconscious, a relationship with our own. We adopt them easily. They may annoy or disturb us and we may dismiss them as being too contrived. Yet they become part of our own fantasy, images we will never forget. One feels that Dali has forced his fantasies onto the canvas and into our minds.

Erotic fantasies are like handwriting or fingerprints. The selection of the subject matter reveals many of the influences that the environment has placed upon the artist, but the colors, the brush work, the way the paint is laid on the canvas—all reveal his personality. The final work sends out its own visual waves to touch the viewer's unconscious being. Francis Picabia, one of the early Dadaists, wrote, "Artists should set down, not things, but emotions produced in our minds by things."

Behind the fantasy the power of the artist's imagination is at work. He is not painting his dreams, but he has searched out images from his fantasies and has made them into his own silent language. Then, combining fantasy and sex, the artist works like a psychologist. He starts with a puzzle and works toward a solution. He is a philosopher of the present, connecting sexual dreams with the reality of sexual contact. He lets the viewer know that he is not alone, that in a fantastic world he and his fantasies can be understood.

Anthropomorphic figures with some resemblance to humans and animals are used to illustrate life's experience. They are seen in terms of human rape, of heterosexual enjoyment, or sodomy, and many reflect homosexuality as well. It is not a monster that hides behind the monumental god but a real man and woman who, perhaps for the first time, can see themselves in relation to their fantasies. The shock of seeing the fantastic images is, upon analysis, the shock of recognition. The surprising images are often peaceful bypasses leading to adventure or perhaps only to security.

The things one wants in fantasy are not always possible to obtain. In many cases the fantasizer does not, in real life, want to live out his fantasies, but everyone wants to be able, without too much risk, to be mentally and physically stimulated. The artist supplies a major ingredient of this modest desire.

A background of buttocks with open-mouthed faces painted over them causes this huge painting to send out erotic shock waves. Recently exhibited in New York, Los Angeles, and Paris, it was painted by Russian émigré Oleg Tselkov who now lives most of the year in Paris.

This is a classic painting defining the magical theatrical world. It was painted by the French master Clovis Trouille in 1944. At left is the section used to advertise the famous musical review Oh! Calcutta! *(Or in French—Oh! What a beautiful ass you have!)*

54

Woman and horse are mixed in the fantastic images of Haruguchi. One of Japan's leading artists in this unique field, he has received high critical acclaim by critics and collectors. Note how gracefully the skeleton of the horse and the body of the woman are joined together.

In a different concept from the skeleton woman on the preceding page, Haruguchi creates a lively filly, half woman, half horse. Stocking and garter form the halter and one sees her spread legs, reclining torso, and head. Her long hair represents the horse's tail.

57

Long famous for his Lolita-like images of young girls, Graham Ovenden of England painted this conservative yet very erotic work. Its eroticism is in the innocent but provocative expressions of the two girls poised on the edge of puberty, their sensuality apparent.

The young California painter Mower-Conner created this sensuous image of a young girl that is reminiscent of Balthus. Her exposed plump legs, short skirt and wrinkled panties help to give her the look of a passionate, petulant girl in her early adolescence.

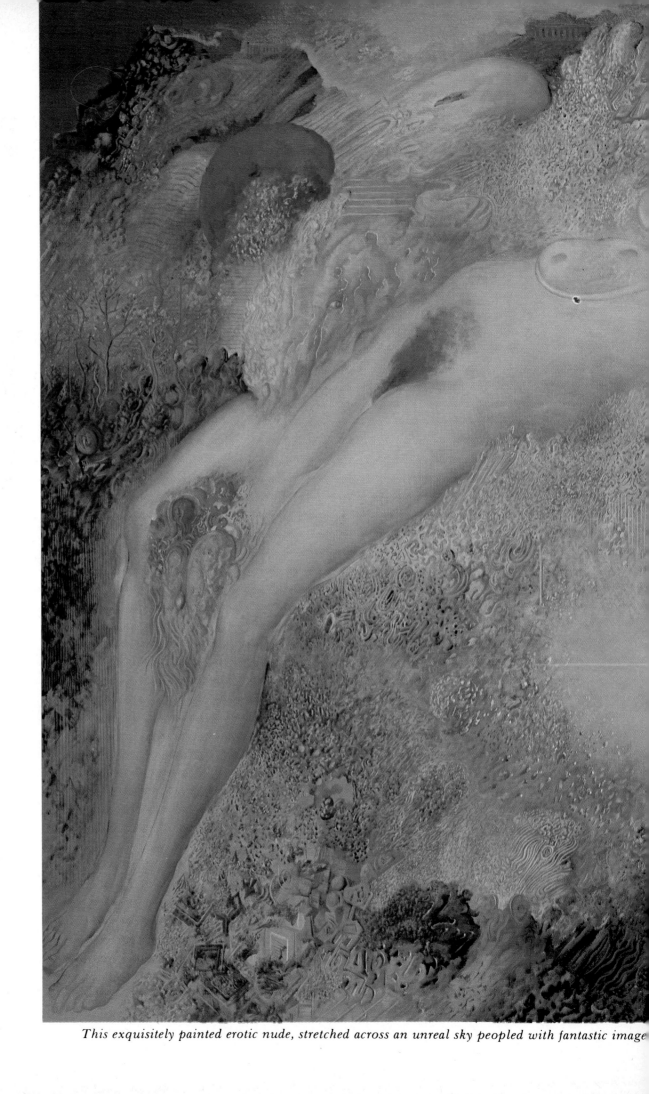

60   *This exquisitely painted erotic nude, stretched across an unreal sky peopled with fantastic image*

ents a veritable cornucopia of fantastic delights. Entitled Le Cri (The Scream), it is the work of Ljuba.

José de Creeft
1940

Daring for its erotic symbols when it was first shown in the 1940's, this work by José de Creeft, an outstanding draftsman and colorist, is representative of his work in the mid-20th century. Titled *Odalisque*, it shows signs of his early interest in Surrealism.

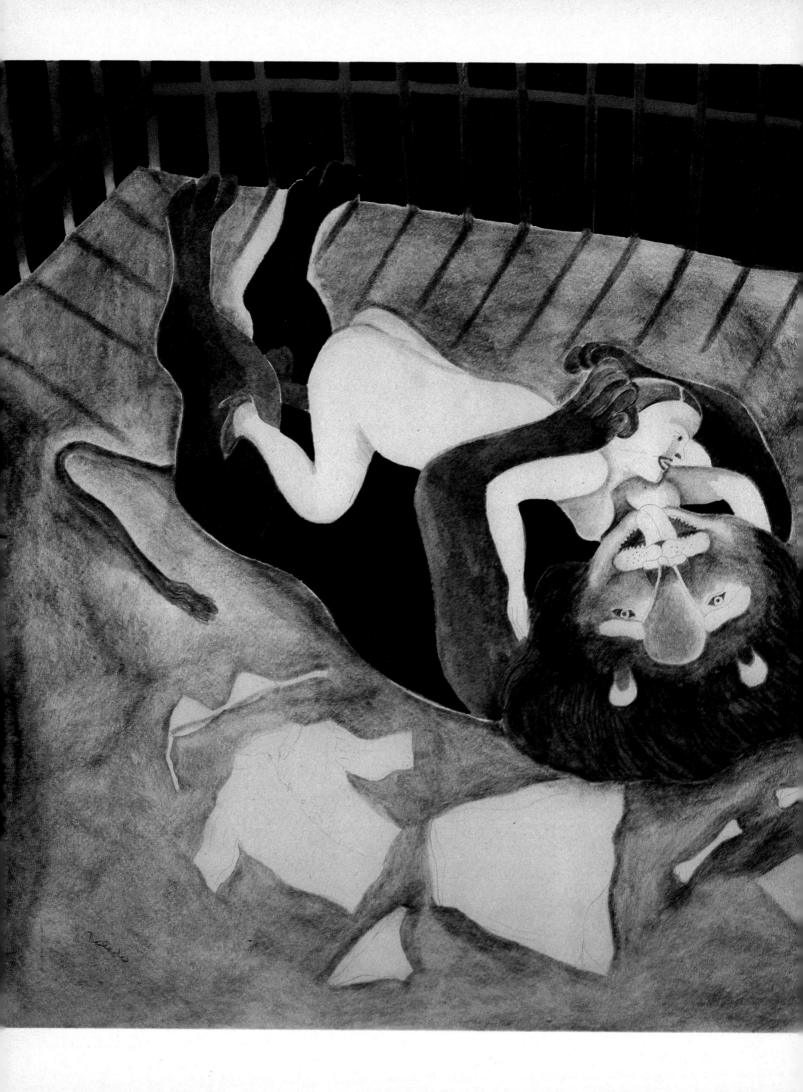

Rather than the lion harming the woman, the woman has dominated the great hairy feline. In Francisco Toledo's painting of the sex scene there is no bestiality, as the gentle lion seems to be the victim of the smaller but more powerful and aggressive female.

65

Surrounded by women, Martha Edelheit has painted herself and her easel in the midst of her "sisters." Unlike the nymphs of the 19th century, Edelheit's women do not seem to need men. She indicates a sexual self-sufficiency, a happy woman-to-woman world.

In this animal-woman fantasy the naked girl has summoned a bear to satisfy her sexually, obviously substituting for a man. Clara Tice, who painted this delightful watercolor, was recognized as the leading woman painter of erotic subjects in the 1920's.

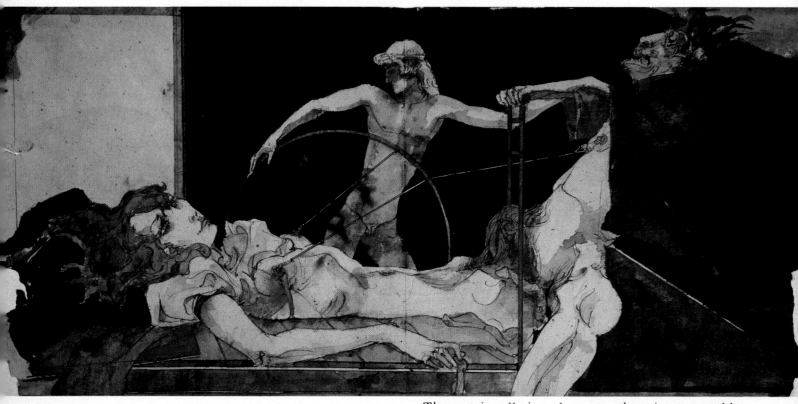

The cosmic suffering of woman, the price extracted by the gods for her sexuality, is the theme for this sympathetic yet painful canvas by German master Horst Janssen. The emotional depth of a woman's sexual trials is on and beneath the surface of this painting.

The young Mexican artist José Luis Cuevas has created this grotesque but compassionate homosexual image. A descendant of the Surrealist movement, Cuevas, who has exhibited in major galleries and museums all over the world, makes his home and paints in Paris.

(Overleaf) A fantasy of sex among the creatures of outer space has been created out of realistic forms and unworldly color by H.R. Giger. One of the most imaginative of modern painters dealing with other worlds, Giger takes the viewer to the darker side of the mind.

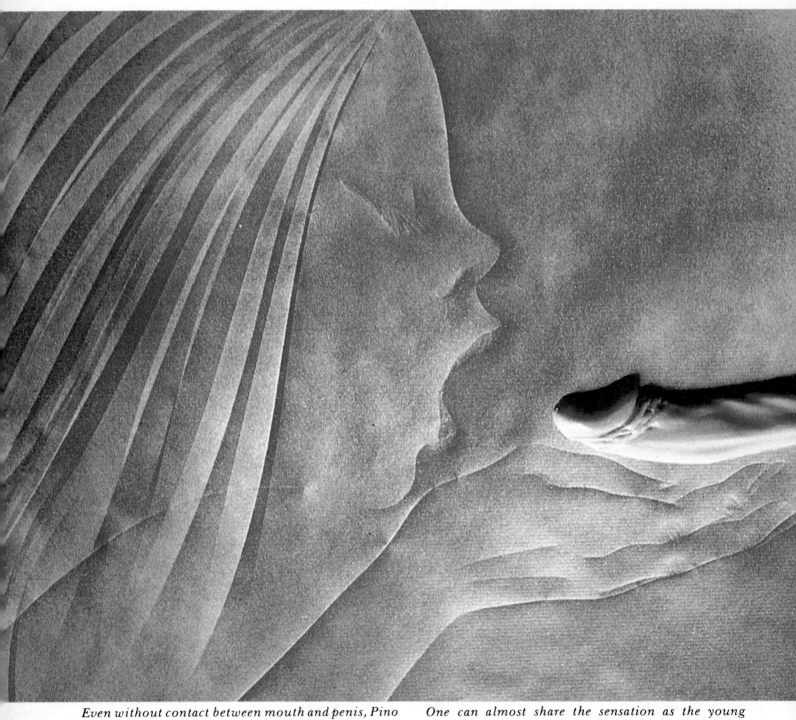

Even without contact between mouth and penis, Pino Zac has above created the sensation of touch. Like a Greek goddess the female seems to be accepting an offering. It is a scene from which both men and women can easily fantasize—as has the artist.

One can almost share the sensation as the young woman at right, gently stroking her clitoris, reaches an orgasm. Shimmering soft reds and greens in the background move with her hand. Pino Zac has painted more than an erotic picture, he has painted a sensation.

(Overleaf) Seven lovely, available women are shown on this canvas, revealing a typical male fantasy. Classically painted by Roland Bourigeaud, it offers a safe but erotic environment. The one man shown at the right in the painting plays a minor part in the action.

Light and shadow, love and violence in Spain are seen in this erotic concept of sex and bullfighting. The French painter Lucien Coutaud has used bulls with their horns as phallic symbols, penetrating the flesh of the women. The matador stands aloof as an observer.

The modesty and warm sensuality of the Spanish woman combine to make this unique portrait erotic. It also demonstrates how the artist Cillero has made the figure more erotic by concealing the breasts and vulva. In spite of the covering one sees beneath it.

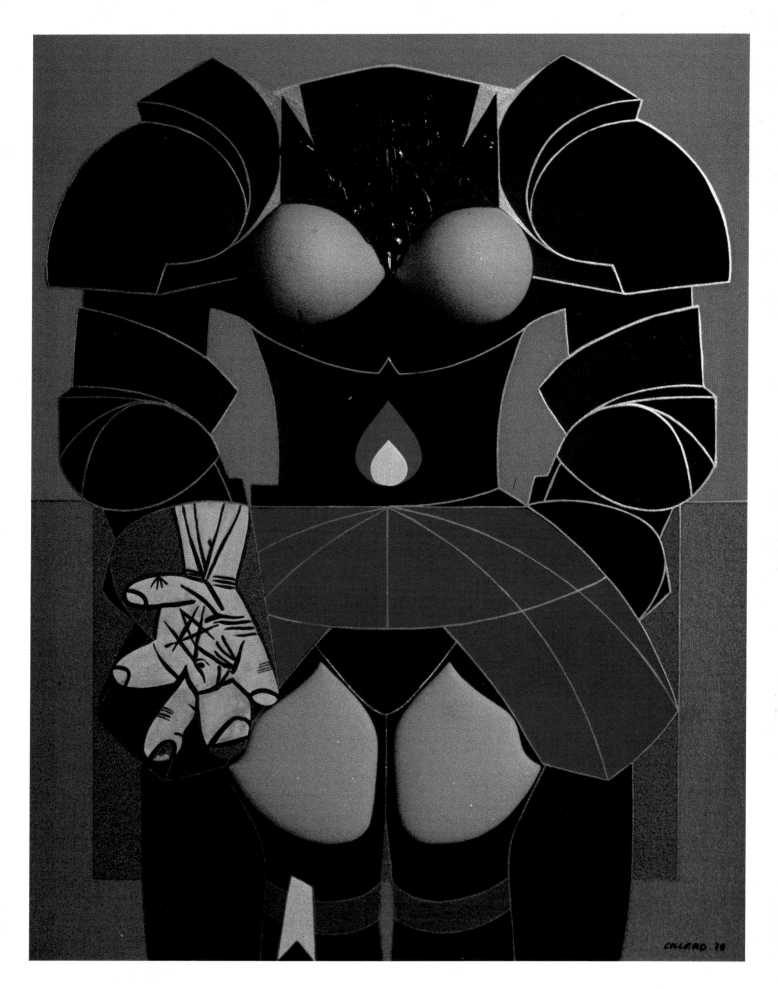

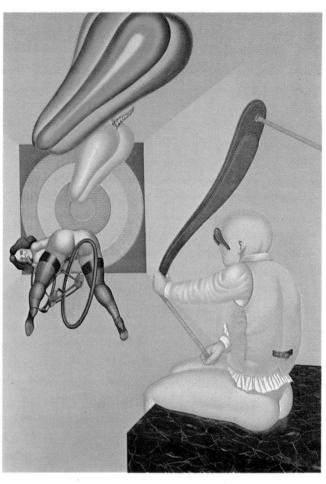

The computer age, outer space, and science fiction are all part of the erotic bag of the contemporary artist Carlos Revilla. In this technological potpourri sexual symbols abound—penises and phallic symbols, strange fruit, anything the viewer could possibly imagine.

79

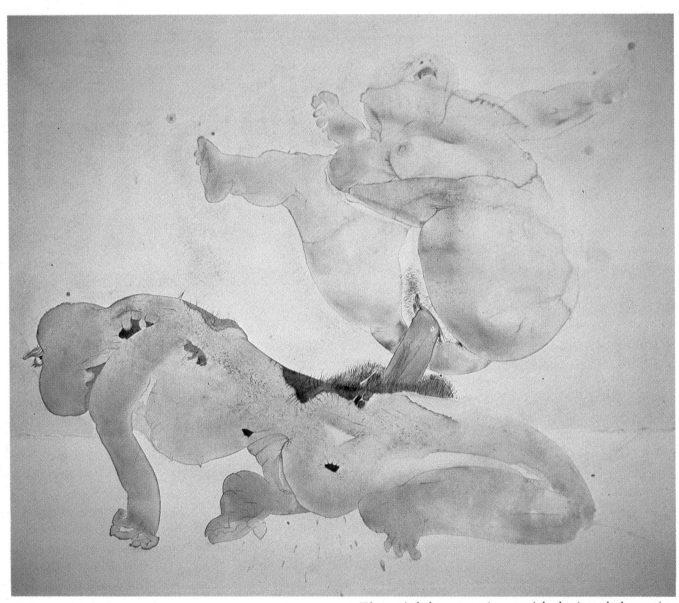

The weightlessness of sex, with the female bouncing off the penis like a balloon, moves this painting into the world of fantasy. Even though the position of the sexual partners is difficult, one can fantasize with the artist Henk Pander in this challenging experiment.

Sex in outer space is another of Dutch-American artist Henk Pander's explorations of weightlessness. Here his male and female astronauts sail into outer space over Pander's Holland homeland. Free-floating in space, common in dreams, is extended into fantasy.

ROMANCE

A joyous simplicity, even innocence, pervades the romantic eroticism of the twentieth century. It differs greatly from the art movement specifically labelled "Romantic" of the late eighteenth and nineteenth centuries, although many significant erotic works were created by nineteenth century romantic artists such as William Blake, Gustave Courbet, Honoré Daumier, J.A.D. Ingres and others (see *Erotic Art of the Masters, the 18th, 19th, and 20th Centuries*).

The early Romantic movement in painting began in 1798 in Germany. Sometimes referred to as Neo-classic, its meaning in essence was that the work did not fall into the field of classic art, art that went back to the Renaissance and beyond.

As a predecessor of the romance seen in contemporary erotica, the earlier meaning is similar to that of today in that the artist's imagination was primary. A poetic breaking away removed it from the more rigid classical form—it was a way of seeing reality through a romantic haze. Poetry had joined painting to form the romantic style. It was not the working out of sexual themes in romantic fashion; rather, just as the Romantic movement of the nineteenth century fired the imagination and reflected the manners and morals of that time, today's romantic erotica attempts to understand the powerful love impulse in order to add poetry and magic to the representation of the sexual image.

Not content with showing the passion of eroticism, the Romantic artist seeks also to reveal the underlying gentleness, the soft sweet sadness, of romantic love. This style of painting is a way of seeing romantically, of visualizing men as well as women in amorous fulfillment.

An important factor in the evolution of Romantic art is the absence of any connection with science. It has a relationship to the human desire for freedom and the poetic enrichment of life, but those changes brought about by science, seen in Cubism, Fauvism, Surrealism, or abstract art, are absent in Romantic art. Painters like Kandinsky, Delaunay, Klee, Rivers, Warhol, Pollock, and Rothko were deeply affected, but some, including Picasso, after allowing science and the machine age to influence them for brief intervals, always returned to the representational erotic concepts. Not even Freud's psychoanalytical theories of sex affected the human element in romantic painting.

The selection of the pictures for this chapter is arbitrary. To the author, the manner in which the pictures are painted holds the concept of romance as much as the subject matter. Sex becomes part of the total scene as does happiness, sorrow, and sometimes hope. Emotion becomes something solid and visible. Movement becomes graceful. In the Romantic category of erotic art there is an outburst of movement flowing with the tenderness as well as the passion and the violence of love and lovemaking. A woman may be fantasized into rounded hills and sensual valleys yet her femininity, her breasts, her belly, her vulva, her thighs, are reflected in this image of the earth. Romantic erotica is both realistic and poetic, but the sexuality is seen undisguised. Although the realistic world still exists, the artist reorganizes it into romantic images.

Though, as we have seen, romantic erotic art is not influenced by modern science and technology, it does indeed relate to mythology and folklore. In it we see references, for example, to the creation legends of Asia wherein the male sexual element seeks out the female. And, of course, early Egyptian, Greek, and Biblical allusions are common.

In the book of Genesis we are given an account of Adam's rib being separated from his body to form woman. We see variations of the same theory of origin in ancient sculpture and rock art. In legend the whole was broken up to form two parts, just as today a pair of lovers *break up* to go their separate ways. In almost every country's mythology the male and female principles, the yin and yang, the penis and the vulva, are described as having once been

A motorcycle, a beautiful naked companion, and a take-off into the sky—what could be more revealing of joyous romance in the last quarter of the 20th century? The American artist Elias Friedensohn created this modern romantic image of today's adventurous youth.

together in one body. After being separated, the two have approached glorious reunification only through sexual acts. A feature of mythological lore becomes a function of evolution. In romantic erotica, the artist carries on the age-old, worldwide effort of living creatures to combine the two entities into one through sexual union.

Both male and female artists have painted subjects in a Romantic style, and by far the preponderance of works by both male and female artists has related to heterosexuality. But in this day of freedom to love, many artists, men and women, have elected to explore homosexual areas and even solo preferences in sex. Nor are artists fettered by their own gender; lesbian and solo sexuality have by no means made up the sole province of female painters, for male artists have also selected lesbian and solo as well as masculine homosexual subject matter. Erotic art in all its manifestations could not be claimed as the exclusive domain of either sex.

Indeed, to the artist of this tender specialty, romance transcends sex. Erotic art is purely the art of love to the Romantic artist. Romance is a definition of physical love, to be treated with warmth, understanding, and respect.

The Romantic attitude is movingly expressed in the way the great Viennese master, Ernst Fuchs, lovingly treats his subjects. Romance is depicted with a reverence that is almost religious. Fuchs obviously understands, appreciates, and encourages romance. In much of his recent work, his evident affection as a male for his opposite sex, and his eminent approval of the two sexes joining together provide us with a visual delight.

Fuchs has shown how the artist translates his own emotions into visual images, integrating these images into a memorable organization with clear, understandable meanings we cannot help but endorse. He demonstrates how the romantic artist creates a world reflecting his time and his understanding within each canvas.

Like the hidden truth to be found in poetry, so the hidden truth in human sexual creativity can be revealed in Romantic erotic painting, more so than in any words or images yet imagined. There is no reason to ask, *What did the artist mean?* Your own interpretation is enough.

The tenderness of young lovers is expressed in this erotic work by the famous Japanese painter Fukui. Working with a subtle yet warm color on his palette, the artist has given life to the post-adolescent boy and girl whose pleasure in each other is clearly defined.

84

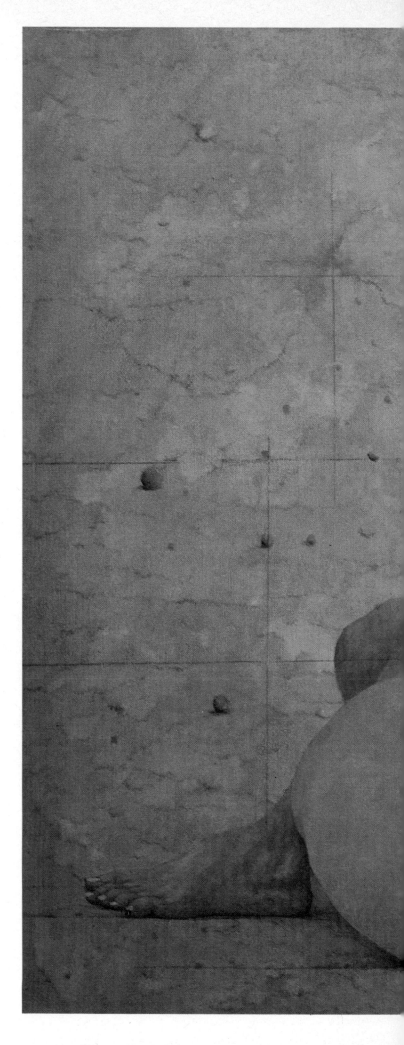

Dance Sketch, 1928

D.H. LAWRENCE

D.H. Lawrence, the English writer and intellectual, believed deeply in the importance of sexuality, the joys of the flesh and the blood. "We should realize we have a blood being, a blood consciousness, a blood soul, complete and apart from the mental and nerve consequences," he wrote. However nonsensical this view may be from a scientific standpoint, it made sense to the tortured romantic trying to tread a path between his intellectual insights and his obsession with a strong sex drive.

Lawrence never stopped trying to balance both of his drives; the struggle made him miserable much of the time. It finally led him from literature into painting, where he allowed his erotic feelings to emerge in a series of strong if somewhat amateurish canvases on the theme of sexuality. In the paintings it is easy to see a reflection of his blonde German wife, Frieda, a long-legged Brunhilde whose real life infidelities he tolerated. It is a little more difficult to identify the smaller, pale, professorial Lawrence as the fiery-haired god on the canvases.

He arranged an exhibition of his work at the Warren Gallery in London. The show opened June 14, 1929, and was an immediate success. However, after complaints of obscenity were made, Scotland Yard descended upon the gallery. Thirteen of the paintings were taken to a police court to be tried; there was even talk of burning them. Augustus John, Sir William Rothenstein and other distinguished art critics offered to testify on behalf of Lawrence's work, but were refused.

The paintings were returned to Lawrence, but he had to promise never to show them in England.

Unlike many writers who have painted, Lawrence was not shy about showing his work. Many of his contemporaries, in fact, thought of him as being egocentric in all regards. Bertrand Russell wrote that Lawrence emphasized sex because it was only during intercourse that he was forced to admit that he was not the only human in the universe.

Lawrence seems to have thought of himself as a simple, natural man. He was not; he was a complex, unnatural genius. His erotic paintings were in keeping with his erotic writing, though certainly not on nearly as high a level of competency. Both were the outgrowth of his own sexual problems. He wrote and painted the way he wanted to be, not the way he was.

Awkward and amateurishly painted, Fight with an
Amazon *by D.H. Lawrence—who signed himself
Lorenzo—nonetheless has power and passion. He and
the woman, doubtless his image of Frieda, his wife, seem
to be clutching at each other as the wolves move in.*

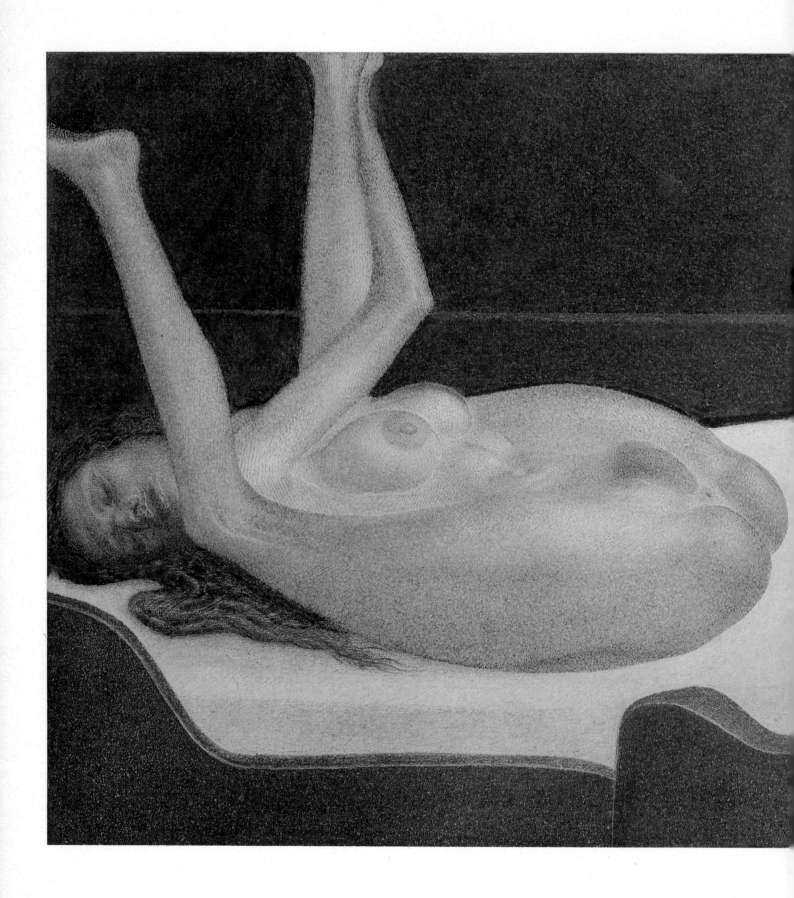

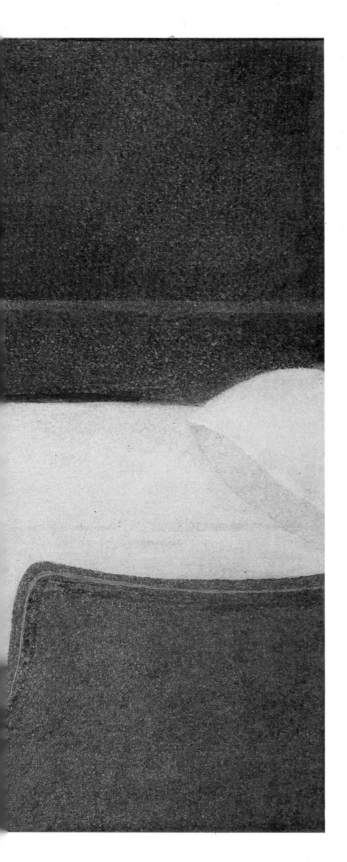

Few artists in any country have been able to paint eroticism with the depth of Vienna's Dr. Ernst Fuchs. A founder of the Fantastic Romantic school of painting, Fuchs occupies an important place among the artists of the world. He has created his own very special universe.

Dancers have long been a favorite subject of Fuchs. Some of his most beautiful models have been members of Vienna's ballet company. In this stimulating painting an ageless dancer with pointed toes floats softly and sensuously through space and time.

A female erotic nude, painted by Ernst Fuchs in 1955, exhibits a permanent feminine charm. Not for Fuchs the trim and boyish figure. His women are long-legged, broad-hipped, full-breasted, arousing in us, with lascivious frankness, an appreciation of their sexuality.

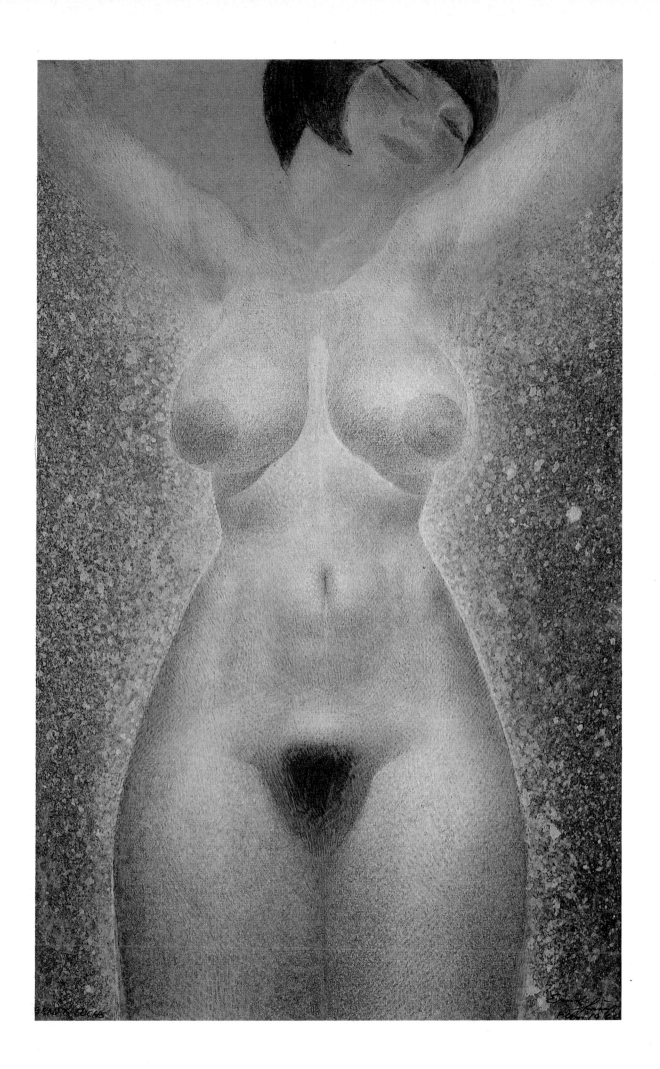

A different and more decadent type of femininity was painted by Egon Schiele, another of Austria's great masters. Schiele painted both lesbians and heterosexuals. He spent months in jail because he revealed more of his subjects than the local censors approved.

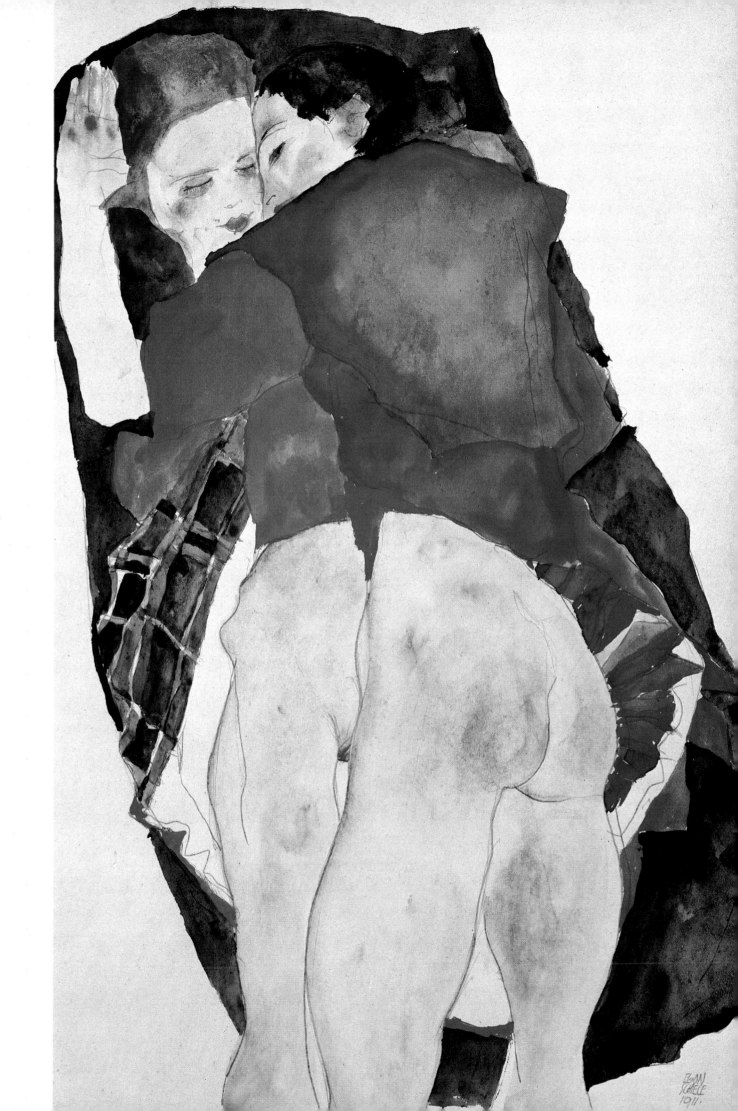

The sculpturesque quality of this intimate studio scene of a painter and his model is not surprising. Giacomo Manzù is one of the world's great sculptor-painters. He is most famous for his bas reliefs on the doors to the holy Basilica of St. Peter's Church in the Eternal City.

This earthy scene of the older man fondling a naked woman is erotically compelling in this evocative painting by the French artist Chabaud. The heavy figures of the workingman and the prostitute are reminiscent of the style used by the French master Georges Rouault.

Les Femmes Tumultueuses (*Effervescent Women*) is the fitting title to this 1968 gouache by Paul Delvaux with its domina

giastic female characters. The two male characters are strangely remote, one wistful, one apparently walking away from it all.

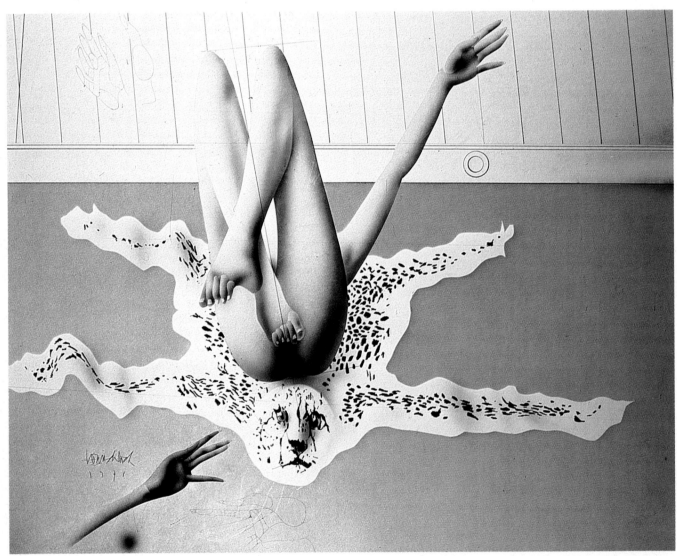

Few modern artists have been as prolific as the German painter-lithographer Paul Wunderlich. Much of his earlier work included violence, but there is an innocent eroticism in this painting of a long-legged, sexually desirable girl lying on a leopard skin rug.

In a recent work (1978), with delicacy and taste, Wunderlich has turned to lesbianism. Although Wunderlich often works from photographs, his finished work has almost no relationship to them. His style has been described as Neo-Surrealistic, with Romantic elements.

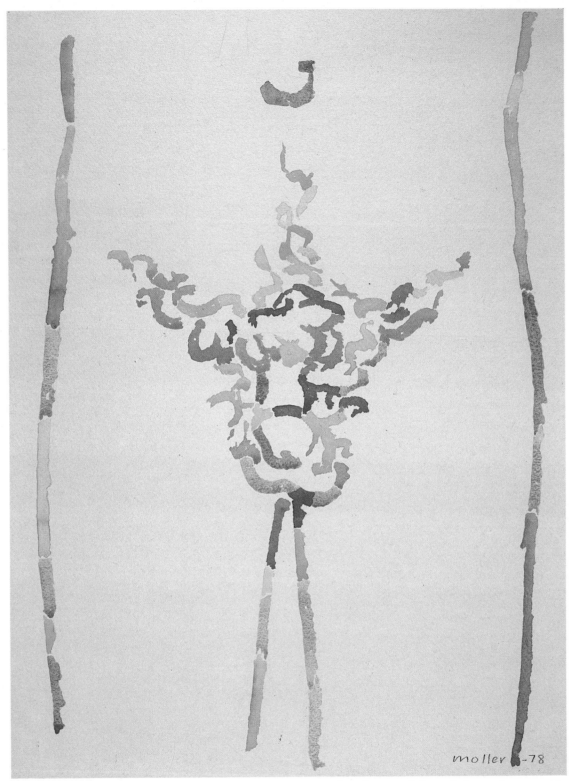

moller 6-78

In this new and welcome vision of the male torso, the
Dutch artist, Hans Moller, has painted a flowerlike
image of penis, scrotum, and pubic hair. The
simplicity and delicate colors of this canvas show the
sensitive rather than the macho side of the male.

A men's Turkish bathhouse during the year 1918 is
the unique setting for this painting which reveals some
of the aspects of homosexual art. Charles Demuth shows
no guilt, no subterfuge in his straightforward treatment
of male to male preference, revolutionary at the time.

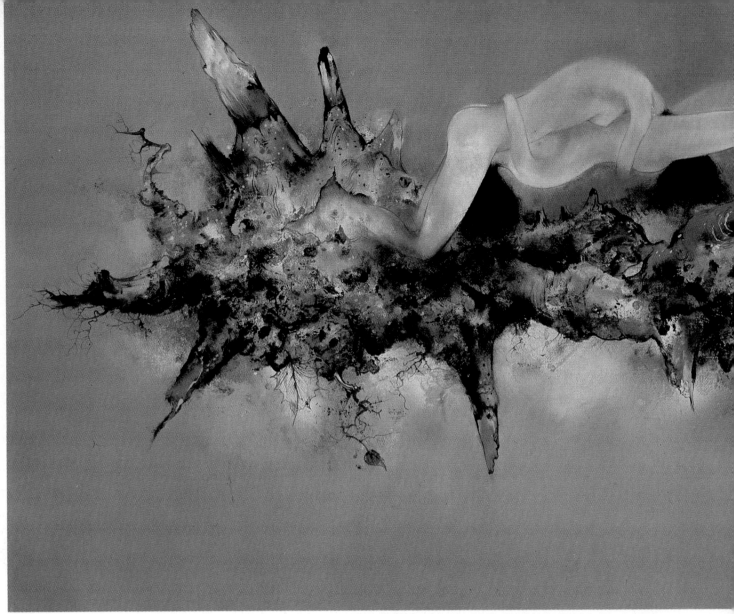

Out of the salt and spray of the restless Atlantic Ocean
come these erotic women created by the French master
Bernard Louedin. In this painting, the women seem
as welded together as the colorful coastal rocks and
the sea creatures that encompass and surround them.

In a rarely seen drawing by Austria's Egon Schiele, the
intimate embrace of lesbian lovers presents the essence
of woman-to-woman sensuality. Schiele died at
twenty-eight at the height of his artistic powers before
gaining financial security or artistic recognition.

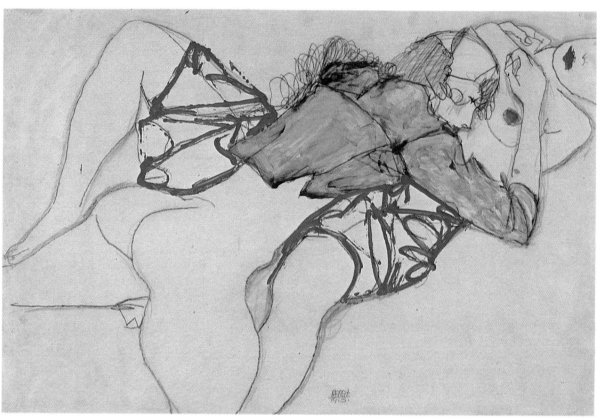

Few naive painters have combined humor with an erotic theme as well as Milinkov of Yugoslavia. In this painting, while his sheep look on with interest, a shepherd celebrates sex with his peasant partner. The elements of the composition lead the eye to the rustic lovers.

In a sylvan setting, these four obviously sensual young females give the impression of longing for some kind of sexual encounter. While one girl is embracing a tree, another, alone, straddles a branch. The German artist Grützke has created a healthy feel of sexuality here.

(Overleaf) Dos Figuras y un Gato (Two Figures and a Cat) is the title of this romantic erotic watercolor painted by Pablo Picasso in Barcelona in his early twenties. It expresses the sexual awareness and drive that kept the artist young into his early nineties.

One of the outstanding painters in the world, the
sensitive Leonor Fini is also one of the leading woman
painters of erotica. A passionate commitment is
apparent in this magnificently painted work showing
two passionate young women on the edge of ecstacy.

Painting with the elegance and taste for which he is
famous, French artist Félix Labisse, in this female
study, has created an understated erotic classic. The
warm flesh tones contrast delightfully with blue-
green leaves and the symbolic blood-red tulip.

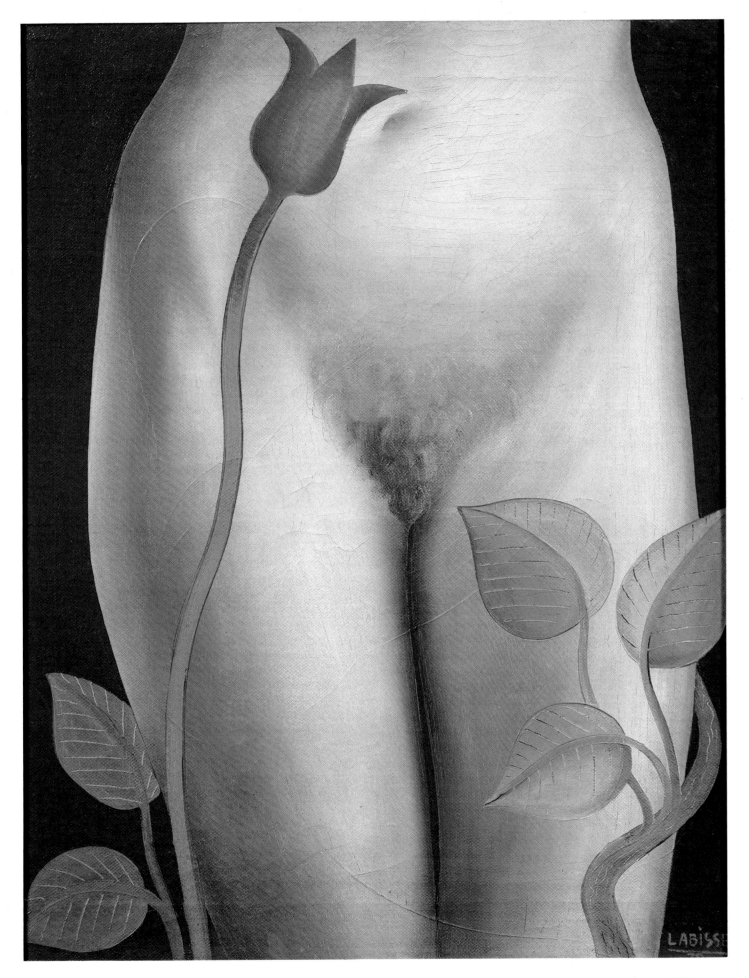

Male and female sensuality burst out of a strange, egg-like universe in Jean Paul Cleren's romantic and symbolic drama of birth, procreation and death. In an eerie and erotic world, Cleren's full-breasted women dominate this stylized painting titled The Dream.

There is a "shall I try it" look in the eyes of the young naked girl as her friend seems to be suggesting sexual intimacy. This haunting portrait is by Karolus Lodenkämper. The suspense is heightened by painting one girl nude, one clothed.

The brilliant use of color adds eroticism to this intimate liaison between two young women. The Dutch-American artist Henk Pander suggests, by the dreamy expressions, intense redness of lips and nipples, and swollen vulva, a satiation of passion.

Few of the living artists can portray sexuality and
innocence so profoundly as the Paris-based Colombian
artist Fernando Botero. This bucolic masterpiece is
simply titled Les Amants. Larger than life, the
characters are nonetheless most believable lovers.

117

SYMBOLS

Modern art is itself a symbol. It probes and reflects a society that is finally coming to grips with its innate sexuality. The artist, too, is a symbol of the new freedom to investigate, to create, to criticize, to deplore, or to applaud his present environment. The artist's very protest against conformity is symbolic of his freedom to create.

Every natural or man-made object can be a symbol. In erotic art symbols are often used for their immediate recognition value. A snake, symbol of the penis, breaks through the canvas (a symbol of the breaking of the hymen). Beside the snake is an apple, a symbol of the first sin. And above these two symbols a woman is seen in the ecstacy of orgasm (page 135). Symbols make up the silent language the painter uses to expand meanings.

In the span of sixty years, between 1920 and 1980, the use of esoteric sexual symbols has decreased. Even more important, standard symbols have been simplified. Within this period of major change in sexual freedom, painters have followed literature in simplifying descriptions. If one was to paraphrase Gertrude Stein's description of a rose written in the 1920's, the painter of today would say, "prick is a prick is a prick," and "cunt is a cunt is a cunt."

Modern erotic art owes much to Sigmund Freud for in his work the dream world and the reality behind the dream became a part of the twentieth century artist's knowledge. In Freud's first book, *The Interpretation of Dreams,* he wrote, "Understanding dreams means understanding a new language which uses pictures instead of words." After Freud a whole new generation of erotic art was born. Artists began to emphasize sexual desires and frustrations through the use of symbols drawn from their own psychic experience rather than from the threadbare religious and military symbols of the past. Modern artists began their comments on contemporary society and probed deeper and deeper into our sexual fantasies and pleasures.

No more the scenes of the harem and the slave market used as excuses for nudity; discarded at last the female religious martyr plunging the knife (penis?) into her bleeding virgin body; forgotten the mythological rapes and romps with nymphs and satyrs. In modern erotica satyrs are men, nymphs are women. Erotic art has freed itself from regional concepts of morality and replaced them with the artist's own ethics. The depiction of the sexuality of men and women as we see them here can be direct yet poetic. The artist can be selective in his use of both ancient and modern symbols.

The fact that this chapter is titled "Symbols" does not mean that it is a discussion of the traditional nineteenth century group of painters known as Symbolists. Symbols have always been used in art, religious and secular. The original Symbolists were reacting against the classical art concepts described by Gustave Courbet—"Art should consist solely of the representation of objects, visual and tangible to the artist." It was in reaction to this doctrine of slavishly copying the visible world that the early Symbolists led by Paul Gaugin revolted. During the latter part of the nineteenth century and the early part of the twentieth the Symbolist movement developed. It had its base in the use of objects and colors juxtaposed to create ideas or impressions. There was no attempt to represent any actual emotion or specific object in the scene. Though a reaction against realism, Symbolism did

Eyes downcast with a symbolic candle, a desirable woman awaits her sexual destiny. Asks Paul Delvaux, the Belgian master of symbolic erotic painting: Who will ascend the steps and open the closed door to her inner being? What awaits her in the lighted room?

not result in abstract painting; rather, artists used readily recognizable symbols and emotionally charged color to create paintings that foreshadowed the coming of the Dadaists and the Surrealists.

Nineteenth century Symbolism resembled the sculpture of India in the twelfth to the fourteenth century in its use of objects to represent concepts. Such sculpture often showed the union of opposites in the same body. Described in the *Rig Veda* is a sculpture of a huge phallus that opens up like a lotus leaf to reveal the female goddess Devi inside. The male symbol has contained the female to represent sexual duality.

In the most primitive societies the basic erotic symbols are the male penis and the female vulva. The earliest stone carvings and rock etchings made by man clearly depict them. But modern art in its creativity has gone far beyond the use of these simple ancient elements. Accepted at last is the pleasure of viewing male and female beauty. Voyeuristic delights are depicted in myriad ways, because we're all voyeurs and because we dare go beyond the outlines of the ancients in exploring the deeper mysteries of male and female sexuality.

Today, the traditional symbols—high towers, walking sticks, candles—are rarely used to represent the male sex. Today's painters show penises, erect or limp, and testicles, tight or pendulous. The anus is no longer represented by a daffodil or an inkblot. Traditional versions of the female vulva—the heart of the flower, many kinds of triangles—are often seen. But their resemblance to the actual vulva is more direct. The sexuality of the woman is exposed, explored in the technique of the painter. Breasts once represented as mountains, cones and balloons are back to breasts, feminine, maternal, beautiful.

There is an important distinction between symbols used as decoration and those used for meaning. Picasso in an early work (pages 108-109) shows two young lovers on a rumpled bed. The bedposts are representations of penises and two penises are intertwined across the headboard, along with several more of various sizes. Yet these are not true symbols. The symbol of sexuality lies in the bed where the nude lovers are caressing one another.

Picasso in a second painting in the same period shows a well-dressed, middle-aged man wearing a vest and looking quite formal while being fellated by a young woman (page 21). His stance and business costume seem to be symbolic of his dominance over the woman. But, actually this is Picasso in high good humor. He loved to make jokes in his paintings. The man in this case is Isidro Nonell y Monturiol, one of Picasso's closest friends and a successful artist who regularly sold paintings to the galleries in Paris before young Picasso had made a sale. Picasso knew him first in Paris, when Nonell gave him the use of his studio in the Rue Gabrielle in Montmartre not far from the Church of Sacré Coeur where Picasso painted for many years. They continued the friendship in Barcelona. It's probable that the older artist had considerable influence upon Picasso's work, particularly his "Blue Period" for Nonell painted the lower classes, especially the gypsies of Spain, and used blue shadows in his paintings. This painting, then, rather than containing some portentous message, is symbolic only of the high spirits of Picasso and of the sexual freedom that he, Nonell and the model enjoyed.

In the pages that follow, symbols are used by different artists in many different ways. There are, for example, references to Jean Cocteau's idea of art as hermaphroditic self-fertilization. There is the actor replacing one mask with another into infinity as a symbol of changing man and his changing personality. Some symbols on these pages can be conceived as puzzles with clues aiding the viewer to find the sexual ideas hidden by the artist. These symbols are, as we've said before, the artist's language. While at times he can project his ideas using traditional visual language, at other times, to create the exact impression, he must compose or even invent a new symbolic vision. For the artist's task is to translate his own emotion into visual meanings and then to integrate these meanings into an organization that finally becomes part of the experience of the viewer.

The human mind feeds on ideas that include mystery and suspense. An empty room offers an opportunity for a sexual liason. What is beyond that closed door? Who waits for me? Is there an attractive lover beyond the door? Does that split apple core depict my lover's vulva; that lighted candle my lover's penis? Is that key a way into a woman's arms, that ring a circle that I will penetrate? Symbols may lead the viewer out of boredom into new and stimulating experiences.

Symbols illustrate delayed sensual activity, the unknown but imagined thrill to come. For movement is suspended by the symbol, not stopped. The object can be defined but the further action takes place in the mind of the viewer of the painting.

Lamberto Camerini painted this enigmatic, carefully composed, amusing look at mother and child in their different erotic worlds. The mother seems unable to see her own nudity or to understand the child's real, however playful, sexual knowledge.

120

Meticulously rendered in the Gothic romantic style, this symbolic bird-woman is the work of the South African artist Louis de Wet, who paints in England. The seemingly innocent image is belied by the dangerous claws and the expression of the model.

In this intriguing version of the Biblical story, Adam in skeletal form has become the serpent while Eve, as the procreator, squeezes life from the apple—which may also represent a scrotum. The artist, Lorenzo Alessandri, has painted a key to life in her right hand.

123

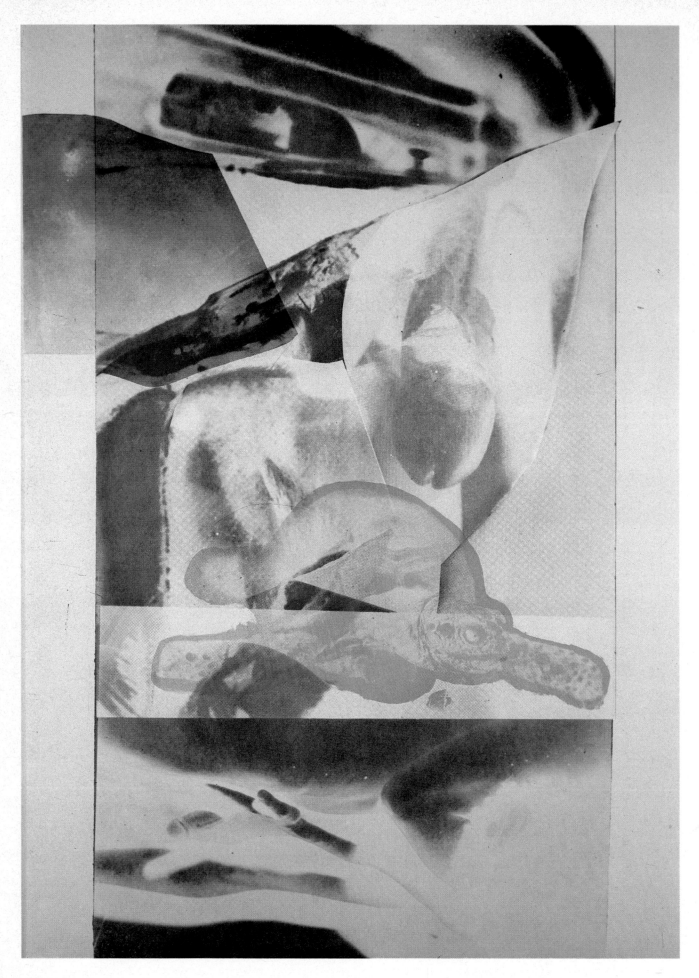

124

Exploring the male symbols, Robert Rauschenberg, internationally acclaimed painter, etcher, and lithographer, has accented the ancient Asian turtle symbol of the penis in this erotic lithograph. He is a widely exhibited innovator in the graphic arts.

In Giant, by Robert Beauchamp, the penis of an unseen Titan projects into the scene to frighten the horse and his witch-like rider. The setting appears to be in outer space; the twisting, bucking horse may also be a symbol of the fear of sexual violence felt by women.

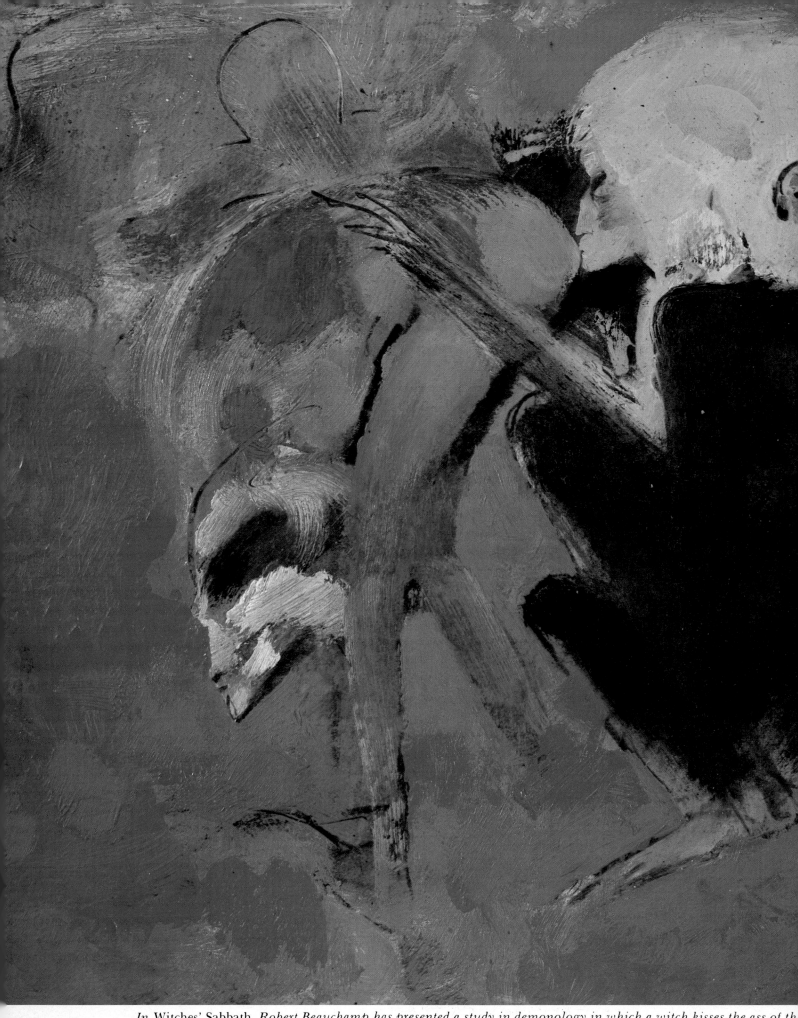

In Witches' Sabbath, *Robert Beauchamp has presented a study in demonology in which a witch kisses the ass of th*

devil according to the ancient symbolic acceptance of Satan as the supreme being.

A woman's torso is outlined by symbols (note the men's shoes and the shaving cream) in this complex collage created by Jane Graverol. By showing the cross section of the rose, the artist gives the effect of endless lips leading from vulva to vagina.

A man with an erection and his partner demonstrate their idealization of a nude woman by carrying her on their shoulders as she defecates a flower. Her physical cleanliness and purity are extolled by more flowers. The title, Gather Ye Rosebuds, by Elias Friedensohn.

A dream woman, her face a flower and her costume and boots out of the past, rises from a barren fantasy world. By masking her face and covering her breasts the artist Roland Bourigeaud has directed the eye of the viewer to her plump, shaved mount of Venus.

Sexual sparks emanate from the contact between this mature couple. Even the woman's hair seems charged with sexual excitement. Symbolic of the male phallus is the red rectangle thrusting into the painting. Jo Heard, the artist, lives in California.

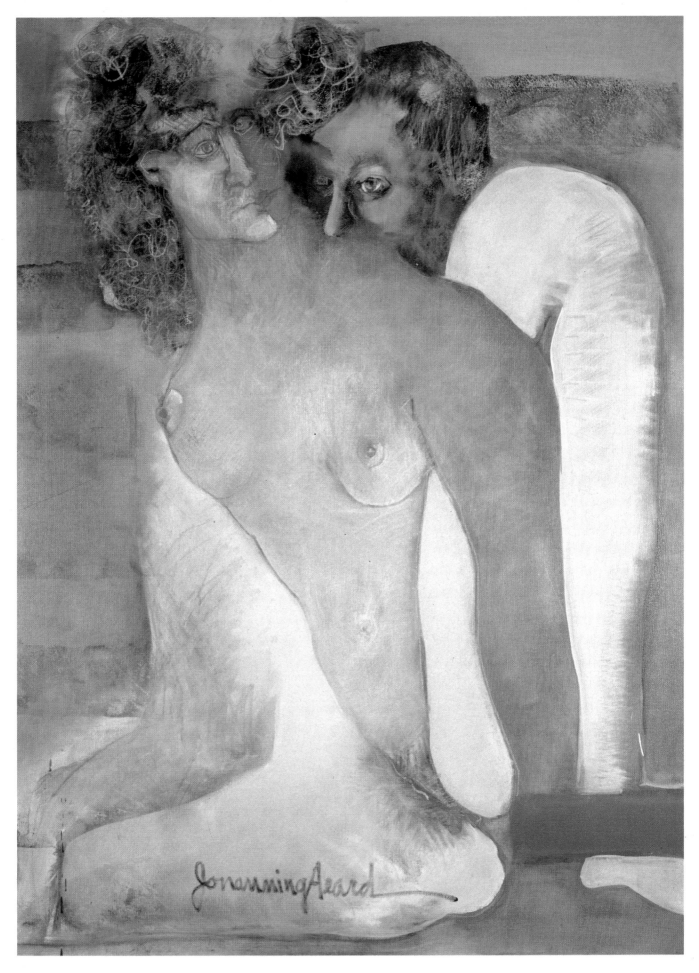

131

All the sexual symbols, bananas, nuts, and ripe cherry are in this painting by Mel Ramos titled Bananasplit.

In a sophisticated work of classical erotica, Eberhard Schlotter has included traditional symbols: the fish (male), the flower (female). On the opposite page a masturbating young woman fantasizes a snake (penis) breaking into her sensual knowledge (apple) of herself.

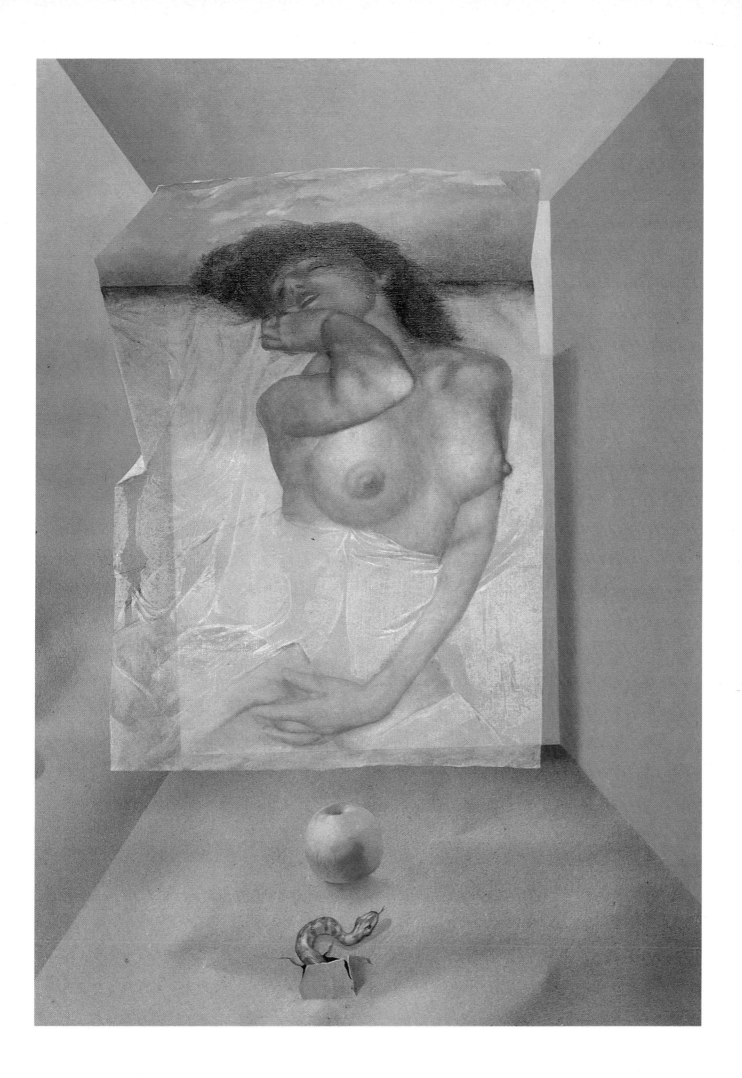

A prisoner of her frustrations, this woman is surrounded by the wreckage of her life. She projects her suppressed sexual desire in this deeply probing painting by artist Karolus Lodenkämper. Like the younger girl on page 114, she seems to be poised on the brink of an adventure.

In a series of male put downs, the French woman artist Bona (Madame André Pieyre de Mandiargues) has her snail-haired female character pushing down the male's erect penis with her foot and blinding him after already having stripped him. The work is called La Double Caresse.

Forty sensuous females dominate this Hieronymus Bosch-like scene painted by Klaus Liebig of Munich. While the women look beautiful and spend their time in lesbian lovemaking, the men; some blindfolded, some masked as butterflies, have to do all the work.

138

Using color to set the mood, Henk Pander has created three sensuous animals. In their eyes, their stance, the three seem sexually related. Symbolically the two leashed animals, one with penis erect, could represent two men out of the woman's fantasy.

In an imaginative, bizarre painting, Alfred Courmes has recreated two mythological characters as erotic symbols. He has placed the Sphinx in a nineteenth century setting while the traveler answers his riddles. The title is Le Sphinx Acétylène.

A direct descendant of the Surrealists and one of the greatest of the symbolic eroticists, Richard Lindner paints with distinctive color and form. In Eve, *painted at mid-century, the ancient symbols become new. Note the flicking tongue of the bold serpent.*

Like master and mistress, Richard Lindner has painted
a benign and dignified lion as head of the household.
His mistress, in her corset and garter belt, appears to
be excessively modest and obedient. German-born artist Richard Lindner has painted in Paris and New York.

This lion is no pussycat, but although he looks fiercely possessive his attractive tamer seems to have him well under control. This amusing, colorful erotic canvas is the work of Foujita, the Japanese artist who has painted a few erotic subjects.

145

By using comic book art as a symbol of the sexuality of the 1960s period, and combining it with the eighteenth century erotic style of India and Persia, the artist Erró has created in montage a distinct image. His flat and pure color adds to the work's overall concept.

Superman has long been recognized as a male sexual symbol. By combining the superman image with an example of eighteenth century Japanese erotica (shunga), the artist Erró reinforces the macho image and clearly defines it in a much broader time frame.

THE NEW REALISM

From Courbet in the mid-nineteenth century to Kacere in the late twentieth, the essence of Realist art has been the selection of the subject. This subject matter is the essential element in all realistic paintings of both the nineteenth and twentieth centuries. It is in the context of the subject matter that yesterday's Realism is always different from today's for, once shown, the Realistic painting becomes history or nostalgia. Of all the painting disciplines, erotic Realism must pinpoint and identify the painter's own time through its subject matter.

On the opposite page, the magnificently painted buttocks with half of the crack exposed stand out as Realism of the late twentieth century and no other. This painting could be put into a time capsule to express the reality of the era in which it was painted. It is a memento of a time when female beauty was very much admired and often publicly exposed. But even in this striking example of the New Realism we see reflections of the past necessary to its development. Realism owes much to Ingres, Delacroix, and Degas. But its greatest debt is to Gustave Courbet who painted each pubic hair and the details of the vulva lips in his once shocking, now historical *Female Torso.*

A major difference between the nineteenth century realism of these artists and the Realist school of the twentieth century lies in the absolute necessity for the artist's personalization of the subject. In an increasingly impersonal society where people have lost much of their individual identity, it is imperative that the artist specify the identity of the subject in his painting. Thus, the modern Realist is unlikely to paint an unidentified nude, but rather a specific unclothed man or woman, an individual who can be identified by name as well as by style. The subject may be a member of the artist's social group, of his family, or even a model, as long as the model reflects a real person in a real environment.

Erotic art is continually rediscovering this identifiable, visible world. The artist searches out a theme representative of his or her special view of reality. This New Realism not only deals with specific identities and places, but considers as well today's values in contrast to the values of the past. Rather than a view of a Degas woman, half hidden by a towel after the bath, one sees instead Carol or Susan lying back luxuriously in her bath, or bikini-ed or nude on a beach. The subject may be in a supermarket, but if it is in that locale you may be sure that the prices will be shown as well as the labels on the cans. Should an artist paint a couple making out in the backseat of a convertible, the car will be accurately identified down to the license plate.

Realistic art develops in a climate of experiment in a mobile society where it is important for some roots to exist. It is the artist who seeks out those roots in our time. Artists create a reality out of the subject that affects them most, making that subject into a permanent image of the period. We can expect those Realist artists of today to paint the realities of today. We can expect them to look inside the complexities of our civilization, to view sex in the context of what is a revolutionary period even when compared with the sexual mores of mid-century. It would not have been possible for the artist in the nineteenth or even the early twentieth century to have painted the female vulva as specifically and yet as lovingly as the Russian-American painter Medvedev-Mead (pages 158 and 159). These are not flowers we see on that canvas; there is no mistaking their identity. And each one is quite distinctive; rather than a generalization of female genitalia these are specific portraits. This painting,

This portrait is also a comment on our culture for in it John Kacere, who paints the environment of our time, has created the illusion of reality. Every detail, every fold, every wrinkle, is important—for this is also a portrait of a tight pair of slacks.

148

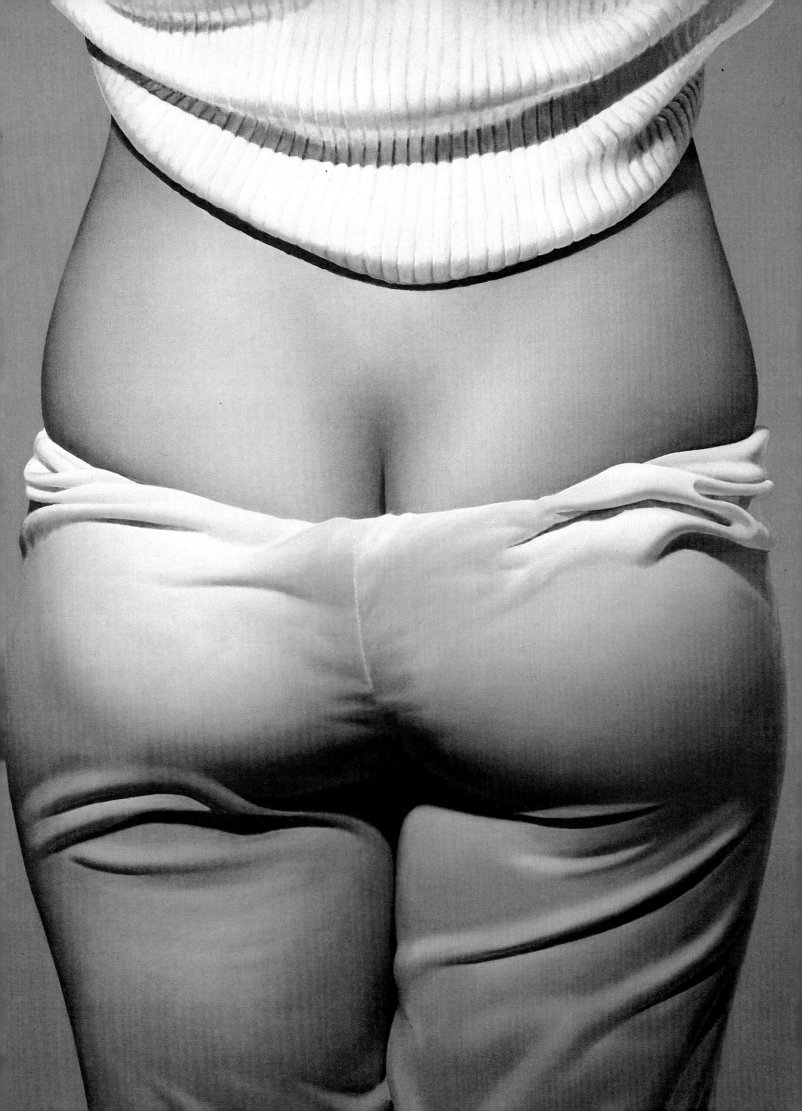

like the sculpture by Mary Frank (page 167), is a form of today's realism. People do make love naked and unashamed. The erotic realists of today know what people do, and they paint what they know.

In this chapter we are dealing almost entirely with paintings that have been or are now being widely exhibited or published. Despite its sexual realism, the painting by Giger (pages 172-173) can be looked at in the 1980s without shock—or *too* adverse a reaction.

However strong an example of Realism, the Giger is not a photograph, though it and some other Realistic paintings do resemble photography. Many have been painted from black and white photographs, for in the approach of some of the modern Realists photographs are often used as a taking-off place. The practice is by no means new; it dates back to the mid-nineteenth century and Realist painters like David, Degas, and Delacroix. Most painters of the Realist School could not help being influenced to some degree by this new scientific development that reproduced reality with lens and film. Rather than killing off the Realistic painting, as many painters feared at the time of the invention, it reinforced the Realistic credo that Realism could inform and change society.

The viewer, seeing a photograph, might say, "Yes, that is the way it looked." But, on viewing a Realistic painting he might say, "Yes, that is the way it *was*." Painting and photography are by no means incompatible, for many painters have become photographers. The American artist, Man Ray, who was influential in the development of both the Dada and Surrealist groups, worked in New York and Paris as photographer and artist, and developed an enviable reputation as both.

Photography owes much to art, for after all, the machine that is the camera requires the eye and mind of the operator of the device. Yet photography has become an important tool of the artist. It supplies a model that does not fidget, sneeze, or tire, at less expense. It allows the artist to work wherever he happens to be with settings, scenery and models from anywhere in the world. It provides a basic pattern to work from so that the artist can concentrate on light, color, tone, and permanence. The modern Realist working with paint and canvas cannot stop the flow of modern life long enough to study its reality; photography freezes the image.

Today's Realists expose today's real scenes and real people. In a culture where mobility is endemic and where "roots" have almost ceased to exist, the artist preserves the people and the signs of his own time. The great modern photographer Henri Cartier-Bresson once coined the phrase, *the exact moment*, to describe his photographs. The artist attempts to go one step farther. He seeks to make that exact moment a lasting part of that time, to give that exact moment not only historical but esthetic permanence.

The artist has placed his model on a public beach, and painted her so realistically that the viewer can almost feel the sand warming her. Artist Hilo Chen has then forced the viewer to perceive and recognize the weight and texture of her full breasts. Title: Beach 52.

In a subtle screen image which heightens reality, the artist Senén Ubiña in Two Centers *has gone directly to the physiological science of sex. The precision that is required in the discipline of New Realism is well illustrated in this geometrically accurate rendition.*

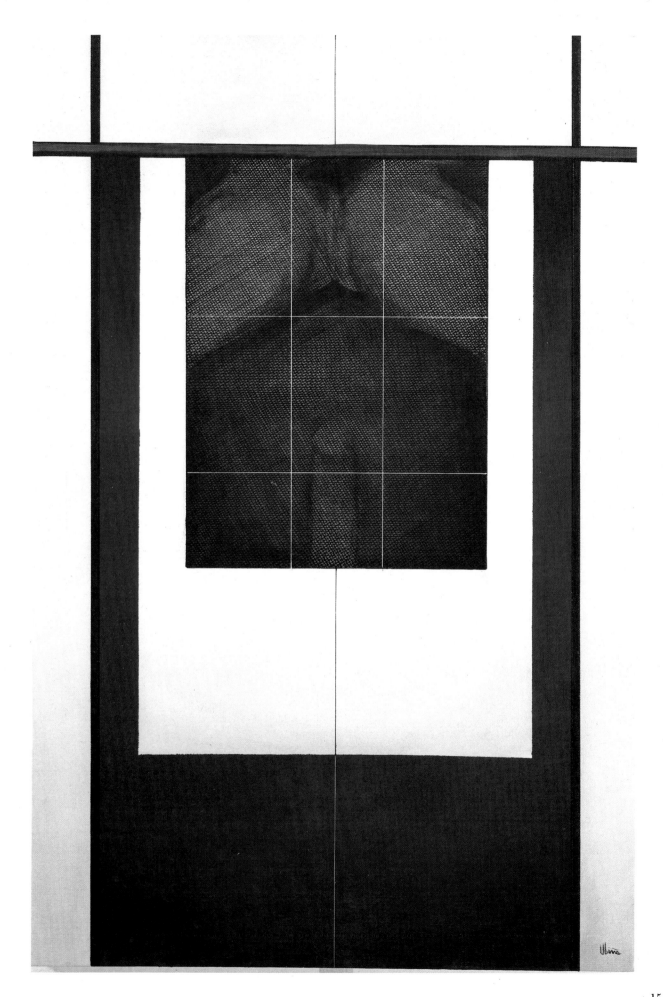

151

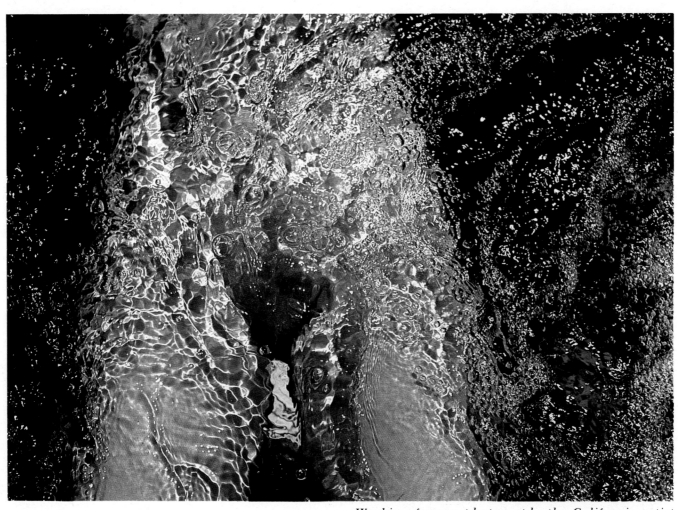

Working from a photograph, the California artist Alain Drarig has created a realistic image of the hips and mons pubis of a woman in a jacuzzi. This is a one of a kind painting, for the distortion and bubble pattern will never be repeated in exact detail.

In his distinctive and modern style, California artist Mel Ramos has piled realism upon realism. He based this new canvas on Albert Marquet's notorious nude painted in the early part of the twentieth century. Titled Marquet's Mannequin, *it was finished in 1979.*

153

The erotic impact of this painting that artist Hilo Chen calls Bedroom 4 is specific. Painted life-size, its effect is so real that there is an impulse to reach out and touch the firm warm flesh. It is a picture that may generate an immediate sexual reaction in the viewer.

(Overleaf) The viewer feels the sensation of wetness on viewing this larger than life-size work (3 by 6 feet). The incredible illusion of seeing a live woman in her bath results from the remarkable surface painting of the Chinese-American artist, Hilo Chen.

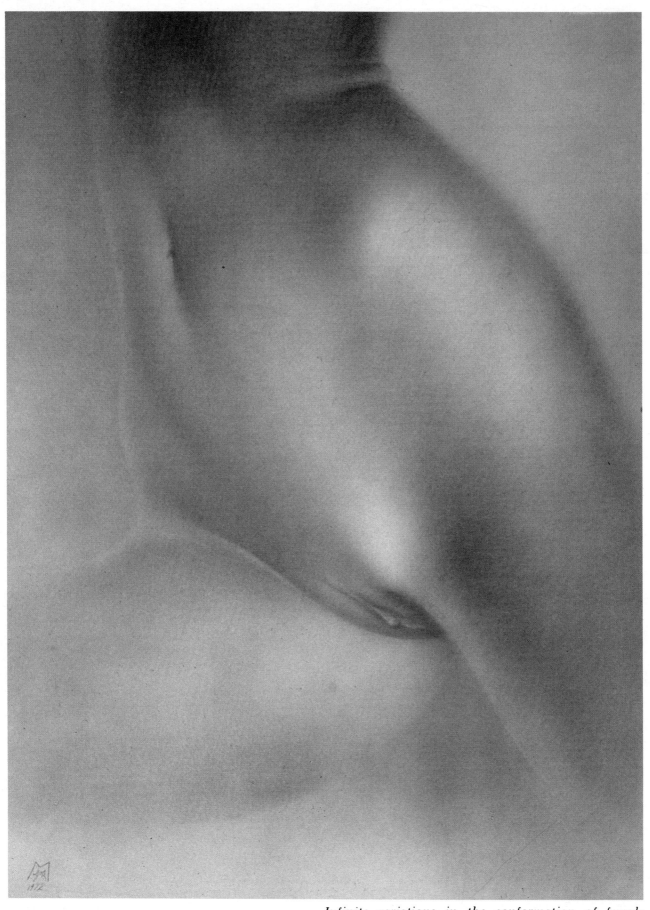

Infinite variations in the conformation of female genitalia are examined in these erotic, physiologically detailed concepts by Igor Mead. A distinguished photographer, he paints from his own photographs, subtly altering them in these meticulous drawings.

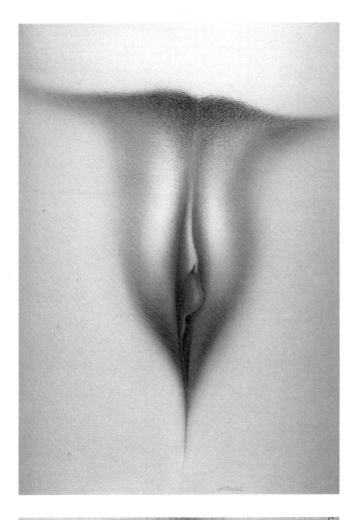
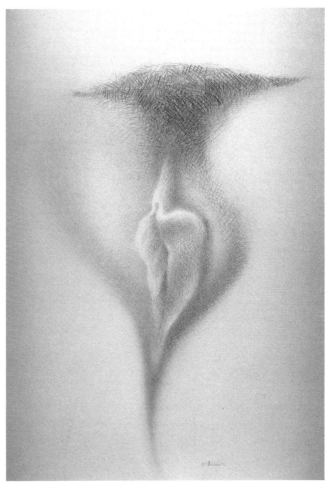
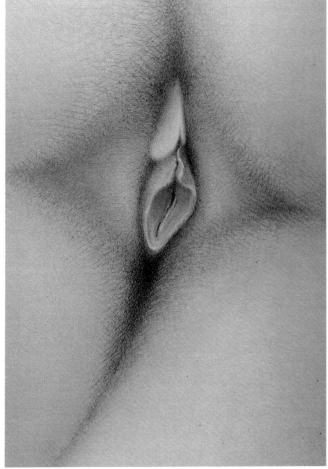

There is a classical permanence in the erotic painting of the American master Tom Wesselman. Internationally acclaimed, he has successfully bridged the gap between Pop Art and today's contemporary scene. Carol Nude *is both exciting and tangible, a modern classic.*

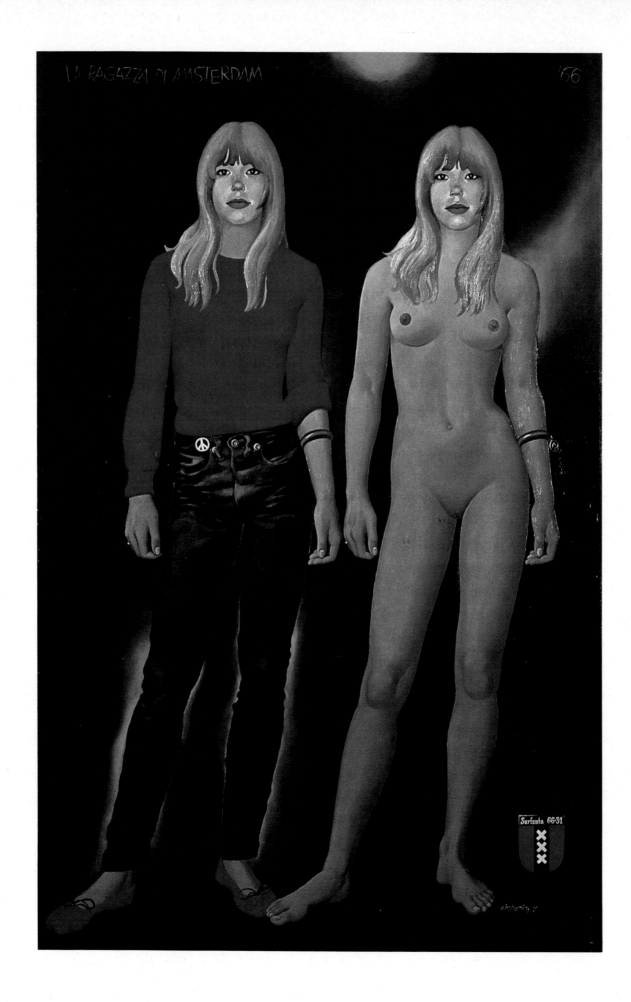

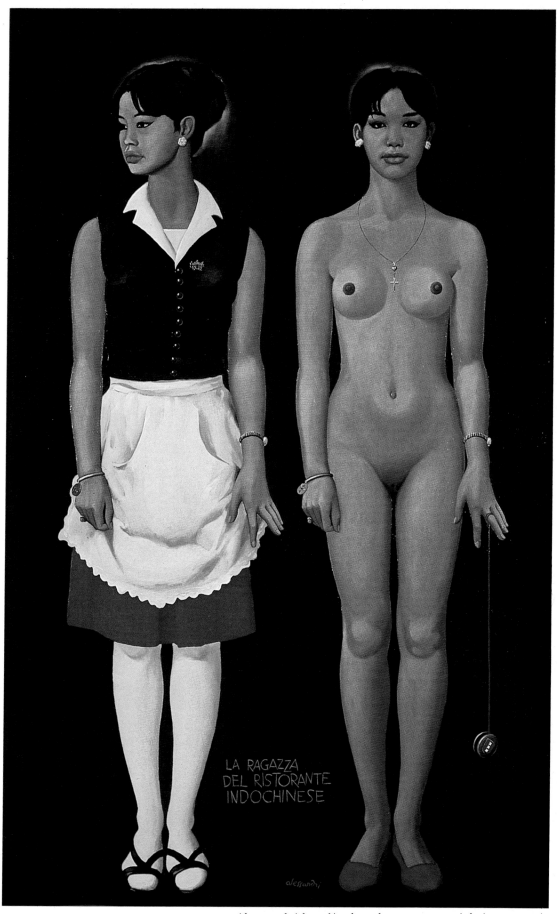

Alessandri has displayed two young girls in an erotic double exposure. The paintings are titled, on the left, The Girl from Amsterdam, *right*, The Girl of the Vietnamese Restaurant. *Note the long legs of the Dutch girl, the long waist of the oriental.*

163

In a Neo-realistic style, the popular French artist
Roland Delcol has painted a young woman from life
(note the difference in the size of her breasts)
grinding coffee in a modern kitchen. The woman at
right may be a standing view of the same model.

With an acute sense of the reality around us, George
Staempfli of New York has created an erotic scene in
such muted colors that they are close to mono-
chrome. The heat of the unseen sun and the Magritte-
blue sky absorbs the figure into the landscape.

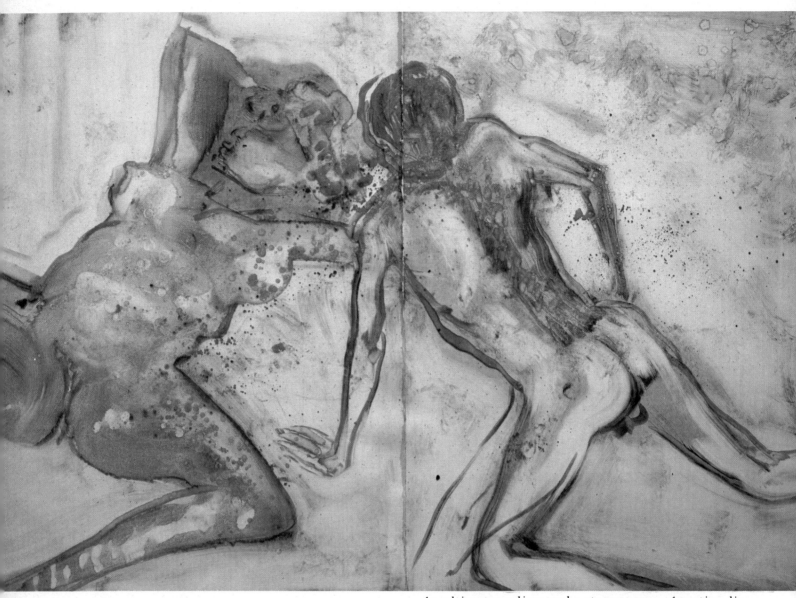

An ultimate realism and a strong sense of motion lie under the surface of this two panel monoprint by Mary Frank. In the erotic ceramic sculpture (right), she displays the same equally impressive sense of style, depth and mobility that we see in the painting.

166

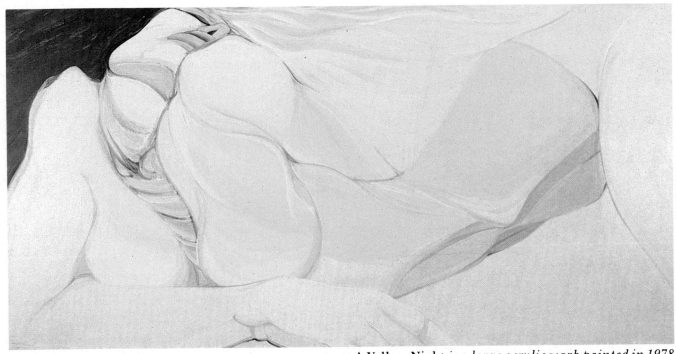

A Yellow Night *is a large acrylic work painted in 1978 by Sassona Sakel, one of the new wave of women painters of erotica. Although complex in concept, an erotic aura emanates from the work as the restless female figure slowly and sensually materializes.*

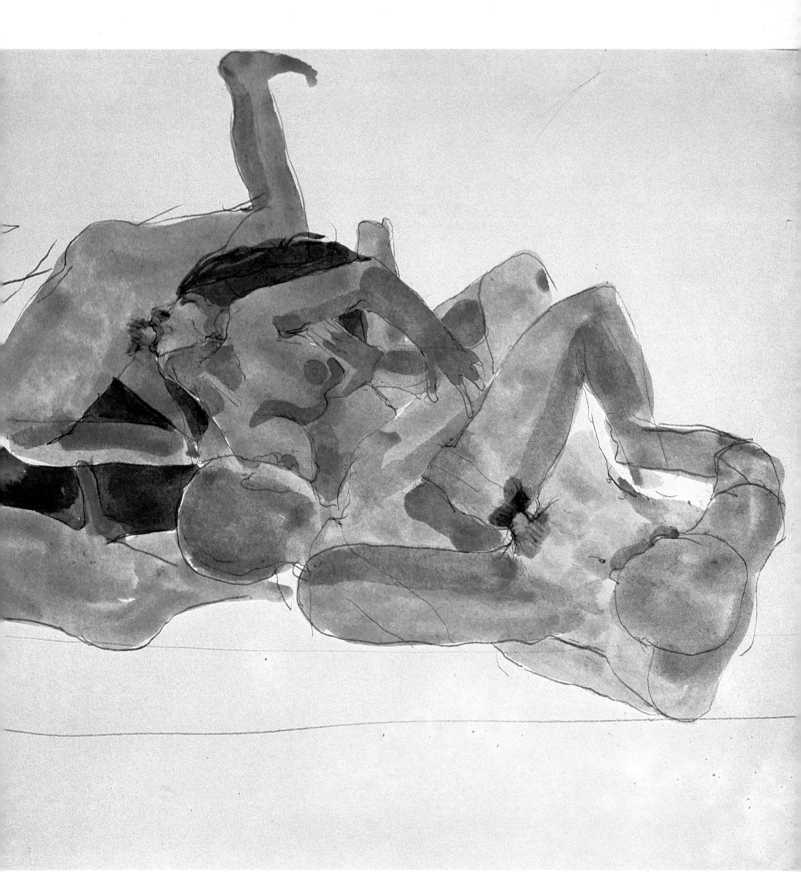

With a definite line and unique sense of color, Robert Parker records a group sex scene that reflects the new sexual freedom. Without comment Parker paints as an observer, his characters indulge but do not react. How many individual bodies can you distinguish?

169

In this Playboy Magazine illustration the artist Martin Hoffman has created an erotic and realistic couple. Th

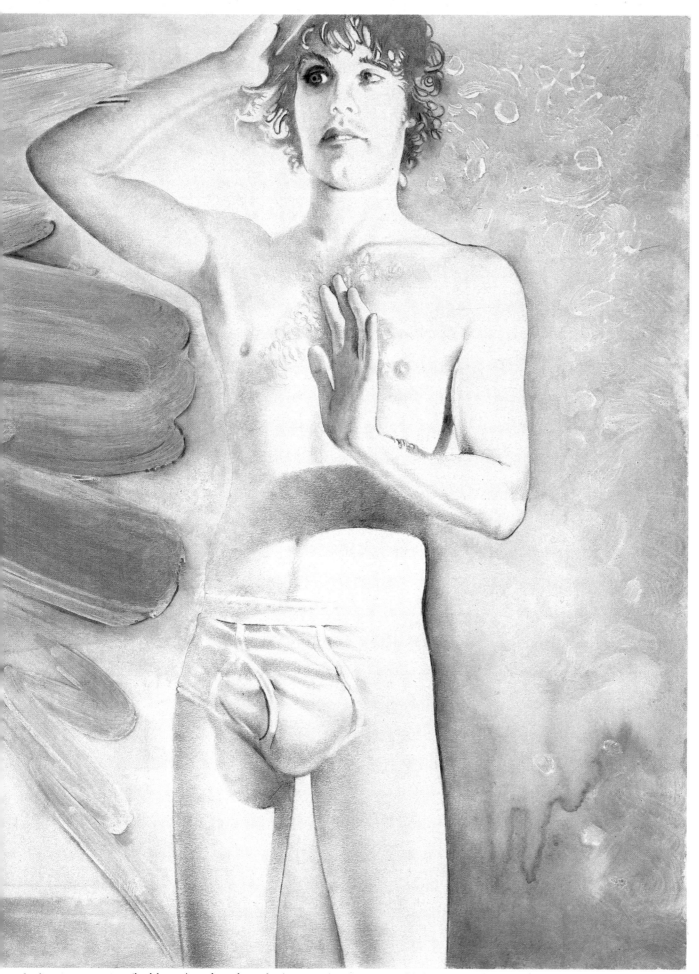

naked young woman holds a time bomb and gives off heat waves which seem to have excited her young companion.

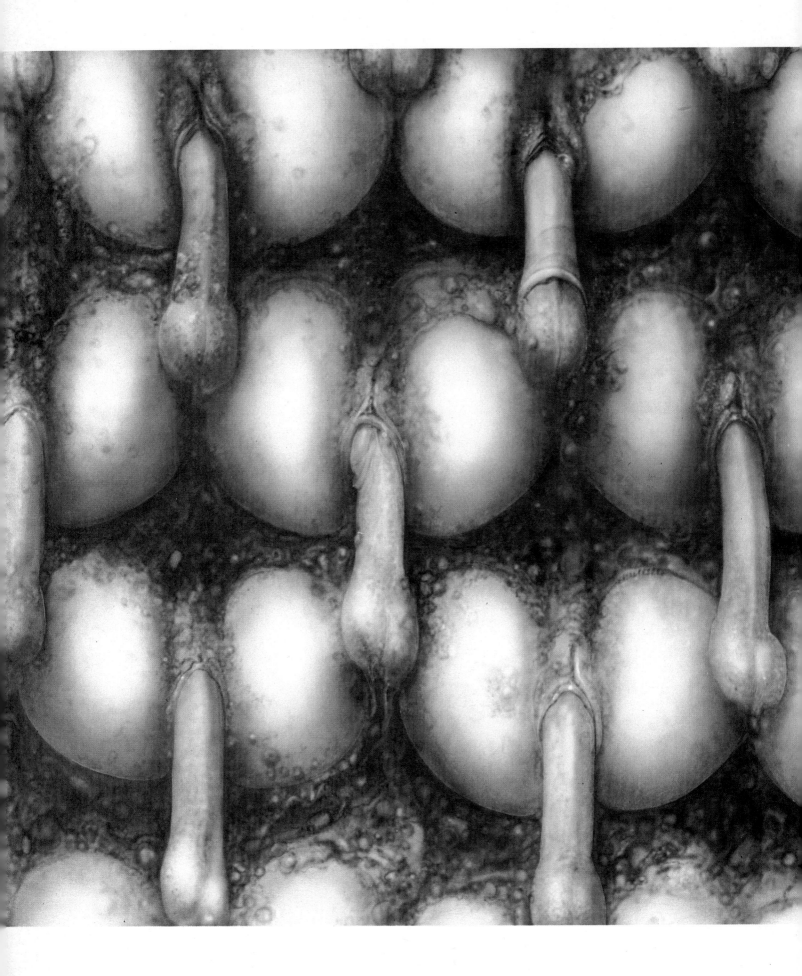

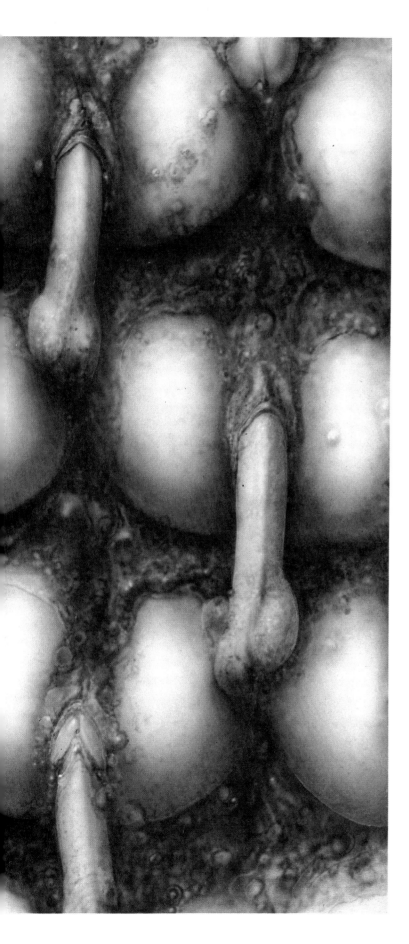

In a direct confrontation with the sexual mores of today, Giger has painted a satire on eroticism. Like the multiple images of mechanical fucking seen in pornographic movies and magazines, Giger makes a definite statement. Note the condom on one penis.

173

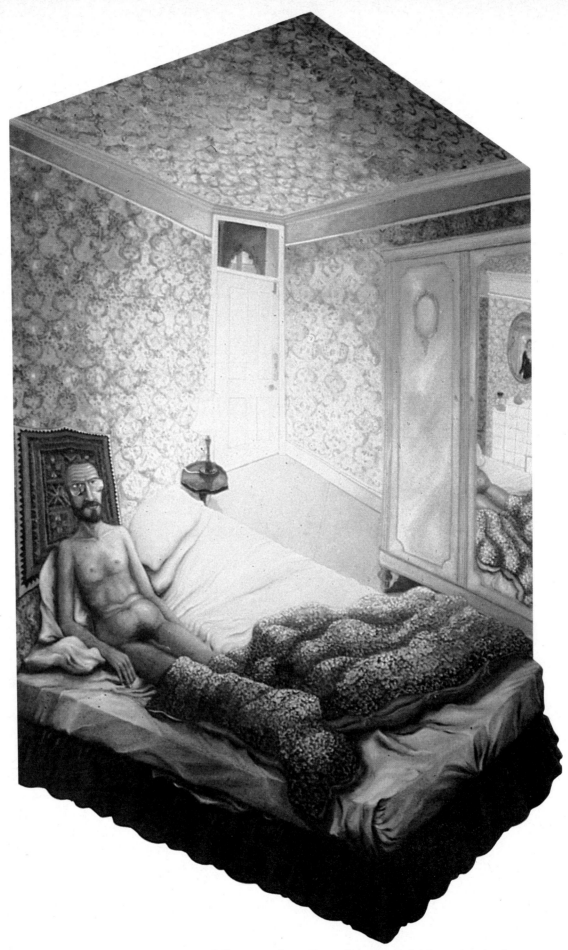

Like a modern Daumier, the British artist Anthony Green leads the observer into the bedroom of a middle-aged, middle-class couple. By showing the entire room (with the wife busy in the bathroom) Green has commented on everyday erotica of an average couple.

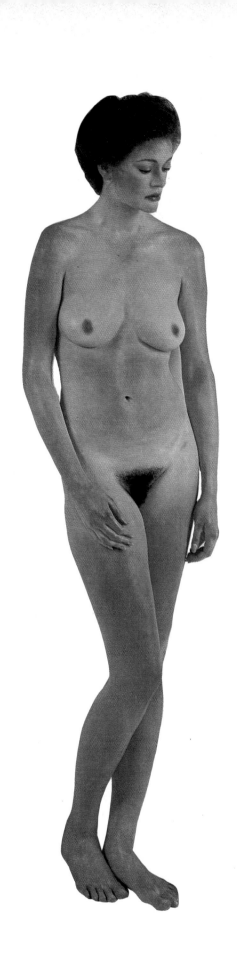

Life-size, life-like figures, these are tangible examples of actual people cloned in plastic and resin. Exhibited in galleries, museums and private collections throughout the world, DeAndrea's people have become a part of our twentieth century environment.

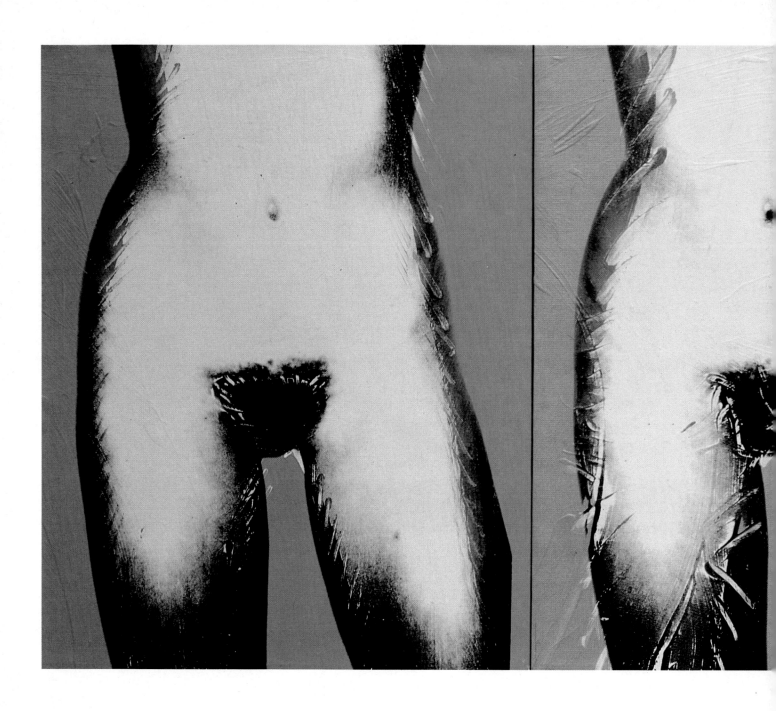

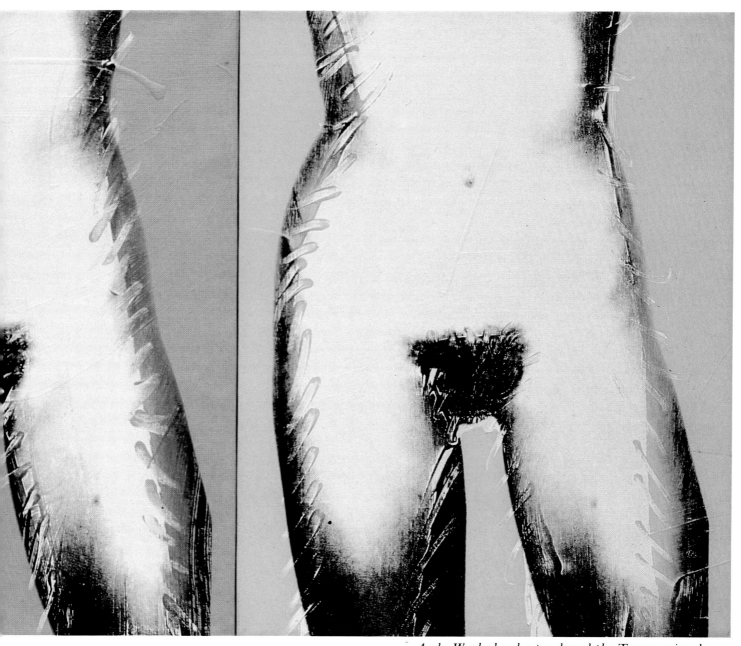

Andy Warhol, who produced the Torso series shown above, is an artist, Realist, and film-maker. In this erotic series he expresses his ideas of sex directly and honestly. Often working with sequential figures, he uses color to point up variations on his sexual theme.

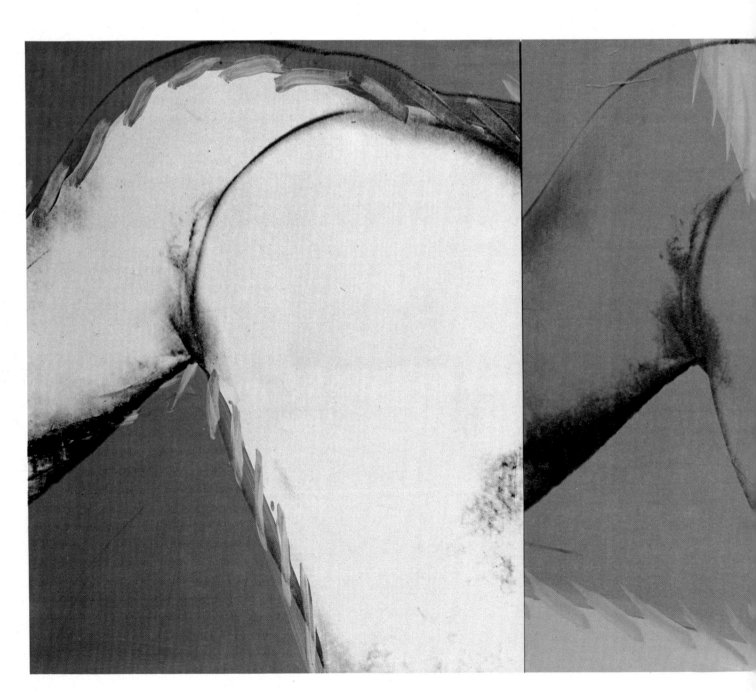

This is a continuation of Warhol's Torso series, a personal statement that is as much a reflection of his present approach as his Campbell soup cans were in the 1960's. Warhol's innovative concept of today's sexuality has outraged many conventional critics.

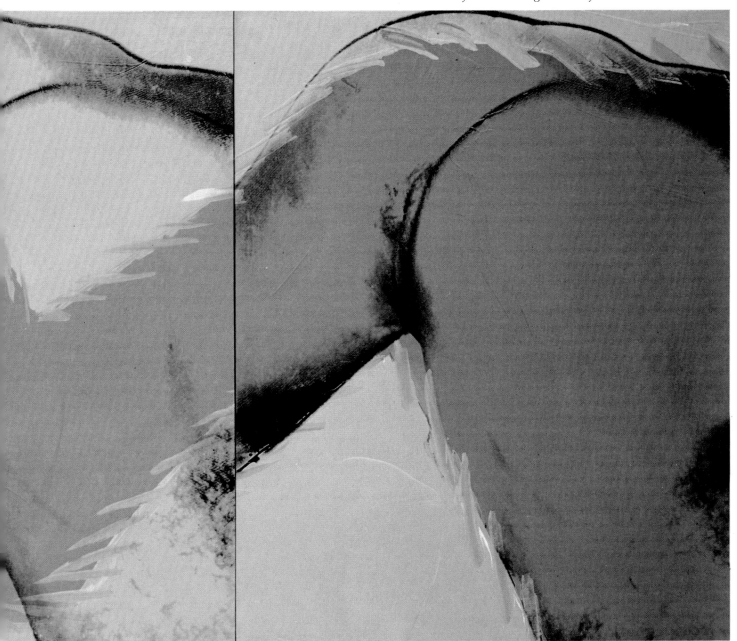

BEYOND REALISM

First there was Dada, an innocent name for the movement initiated by a revolutionary group of artists and writers who shook up the culture of the early twentieth century so violently that it has, fortunately, never recovered.

Until Dada, classical traditional art had sailed smoothly along for some time, disturbed only by storms painted up by Goya in his last years, Van Gogh in his short painting life, and Paul Gauguin. Then, in 1915, the fireworks began. The explosions were ignited by a then unknown but talented handful of misfits in Zurich, Paris, and New York. The New York contingent under the dramatic black cloak of photographer-impresario Alfred Steiglitz included Francis Picabia, photographer-artist Man Ray, and the unpredictable young French artist Marcel Duchamp.

When in that year, Duchamp drew a moustache and beard on Leonardo DaVinci's *Mona Lisa*, he struck a never to be forgotten blow against conventional painting. In inscribing the letters L.H.O.O.Q. on the altered portrait, he made a major protest against censorship—for these letters spoken rapidly in French sound like *"Elle a chaud au cul"* or *"She's got a hot ass."* Some fifty years later, incidentally, a painting by French artist Clovis Trouille (pages 54-55), who was not a Dadaist, was used to promote an all nude Broadway spectacle called *Oh! Calcutta!* Pronounced slowly in French it translates as *"Oh quel cul t'as,"* ("Oh what an ass you have").

With this protest Duchamp became a triple threat man of the arts. At one and the same time he was attacking the pretensions of classical art, defying current censorship, and commenting on DaVinci's homo- or bisexuality.

The aims of the Dadaists were largely destructive. In order to put down pretentious cultural attitudes they strove to destroy all traditional art up to the time of their birth. Artists talented to the point of genius, they wielded the powerful weapons of satire and ridicule.

Duchamp had made a striking Dada visual statement long before the moustached *Mona Lisa*. His painting, *Nude Descending a Staircase*, created seven years earlier, had an electrifying effect upon the respectable art community when it was seen in Paris. Taken to New York, it created an immediate and shocking effect on viewers and critics there. It was not criticized for its sexuality, as the symbols were difficult to detect, but because its cubistic, fragmented technique did not fit into the preconceived notion of what representational art should be. Duchamp replied to scornful critics with the cheerful statement that, "Most people, being used to seeing nudes lying down or standing up, were naturally shocked to see one walking down a staircase."

His friend, Man Ray, wrote, "Strange how those most suspicious of your pulling their legs haven't any to stand on." The painting was purchased by a San Francisco art dealer for $324. Its present value is in excess of half a million.

Other Dadaists who greatly influenced modern erotic art include the Zurich group, Jean Arp, Hugo Ball, and Tristan Tzara. By 1919, Kurt Schwitters and Max Ernst had also become important members. They combined forces in Dada's mission of destroying traditional art. Some advocated the performance of the spontaneous act to reveal the illogic of conventional order, though not all went as far as the Dada hero, Arthur Craven, who interrupted a staid lecture at the Salle des Sociétés by shooting a pistol repeatedly into the air. Tristan Tzara, in a joint statement with the French poet Apollinaire and painter Jean Arp, held that each Dada act was a cerebral revolver shot. A half century later, the Dadaist's dramatizations came around

This electronic fucking machine, photographed in the studio of artist Larry Rivers, would have delighted early Surrealists. Lights flashing, glowing penis and female body move together in this satire of pinballs and Masters and Johnson laboratory experiments.

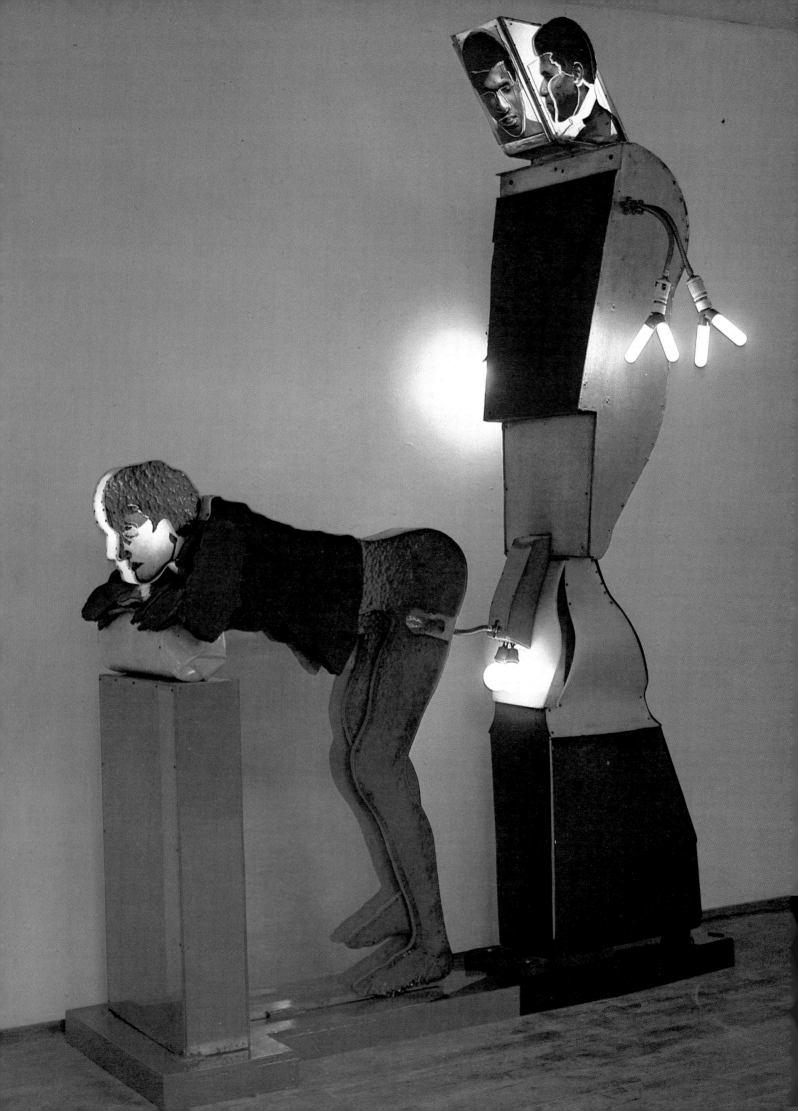

again in the "Happenings" of the 1960s and 1970s.

Out of the mad and unpredictable world of Dada came a new discipline. Called Surrealism, it was named by Apollinaire who wrote, "After thinking, I prefer to adapt the word Surréalisme rather than the Surnaturalisme I used at first." In a fragment of a poem written at the time, he said, "Now the time comes when you are bored with antiquity...You have had enough of life in the Greek and Roman world."

Both Surrealism and eroticism were of great importance to Apollinaire. He prepared new editions and wrote prefaces for the then infamous works of the Marquis de Sade, Aretino, and Baudelaire, and for *Fanny Hill,* and the *Erotika Biblion* of the Comte de Mirabeau.

The influence and poetry of Apollinaire were not enough to launch the Surrealists. It was André Breton, philosopher-writer and dedicated cultural revolutionary (with assists from Sigmund Freud, Carl Jung, André Masson, Salvador Dali, Max Ernst, Matta Echaurren the Chilean painter, Jean Cocteau, and Jean Arp), whose passion for the Surrealist idea made it an international influence in twentieth century art.

Major artists throughout the western world were deeply influenced by both the intellectual and visual discipline of Surrealism. Picasso, while never an official member of the movement, attended meetings regularly. He admitted many times that his work had been influenced by the Surrealists, and in 1941 wrote a Surrealist play, *Desire Caught By The Tail.* The sense of the play was not caught by the audience, possibly because the author had incorporated automatic writing in its creation. It has rarely been replayed.

For all the Surrealist influence, it would be a mistake to call Picasso's work Surrealist or Cubist, or indeed to try to label it at all. For Picasso's style, it was said, changed with his women while Cocteau's style changed with his men.

It was inevitable that Surrealism would mark the end of Cubism. With a structure directly opposite to that of the Surrealists, Cubism was a rational concept, a way of seeing all sides of the subject at once. On the other hand, Surrealism was, according to Breton, "Pure psychic automatism...by which it is intended to express, either verbally or in writing, the true function of thought...thought dictated in the absence of all control dictated by reason, and outside all esthetic or moral preoccupations."

The Surrealists believed that to reach beyond reality should be not only the aim of the artist but of the viewer as well. Surrealism, however, is not a realm of unreality, nor one of fantasy or of dreams, although it embraces all three. Rather it is a world of perception learned through the subconscious.

The thrust of the Surrealists has persisted into the 1980s. To a high degree those artists and writers whose work still illuminates the world, as well as their young descendants, achieved many of their original aims. The depth and popularity of their work helped to abolish censorship. And the visualization of human desire and physical love now acceptable in the galleries and museums is part of their heritage.

But the Surrealists have been responsible for much more in terms of human sexual fulfillment, by showing emotions from within, by addressing their art to the myriad sexual problems and pleasures, by illustrating human fantasies and reducing those fantasies to reality, by exposing the cruelty and violence as well as the ecstasy of love. The Surrealists, and their descendants, have acted as visual psychiatrists to the modern ocular world.

Later twentieth century descendants of the Surrealists, painters Rauschenberg, Rivers, Frank, Kitaj, Cuevas, Merkin, Ting, Revilla, and Ljuba, among others, continued the tradition of pattern breaking. Unlike the Surrealists, they have not joined a movement, but found their individual insights without recourse to rules. They have insisted upon their right to be irrational in an irrational world. Modern artists have not allowed civilization to stand still or to become classically sterile; one new wave breaks upon another, uncovering still more visual ways to move toward human understanding.

Our comfortable respectable ways of life are continually under the probing mind and eye of the modern artist who sees beyond today. Reality as we see it is replaced by an unfamiliar and often uncomfortable set of images. Looking at contemporary erotic painting a viewer may say that the artist is irresponsible, possibly even insane. But soon the viewer will catch up, will perceive the artist's insights. And when he does, the artist will then take off again into an unpredictable future world. This game of catch up has been played in art as in life continuously throughout the twentieth century. One must learn to look beyond reality to find life's elusive meanings.

Motion and eroticism are evoked with an economy of line and color in this watercolor, Dancer, *by the French master André Masson. The attitude of the nude dancer, the flow of her hair, her graceful foot movement, all go to complete this classic composition.*

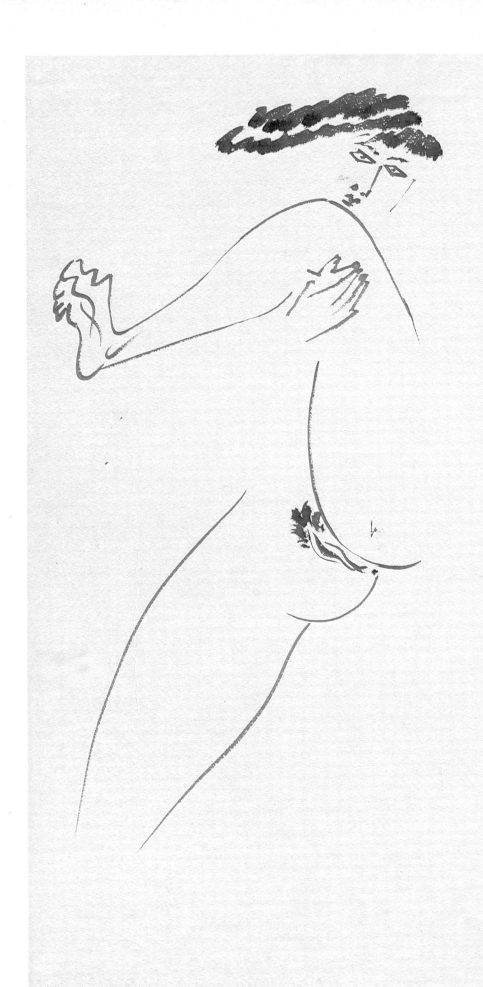

Automatic painting, in which the hand and mind of the artist were allowed to roam freely, was one of the first disciplines of the Surrealists. In this lithograph, André Masson's talented hand and eye lead the viewer through a serpentine labyrinth of colorful sexuality.

184

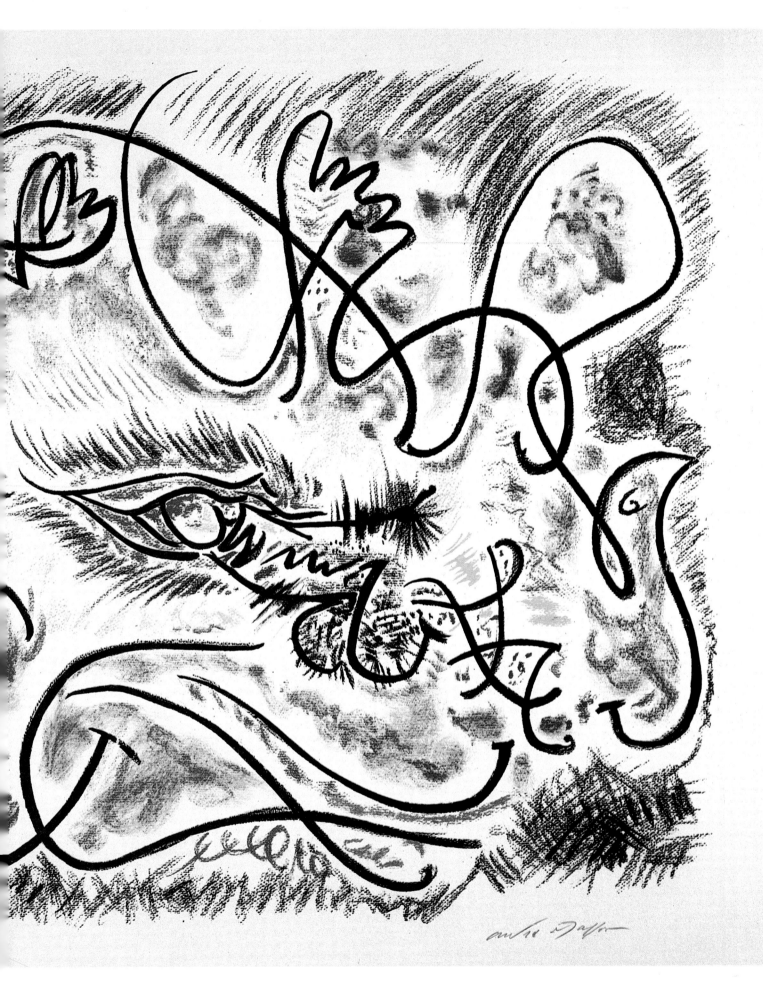

DALI EROTICA

Salvador Dali has, it seems to me, been criticized for all the wrong reasons—for calling attention to himself and his work, for wearing a long moustache, for painting too technically well, and for making too much money. He has, in short, been accused of the sin of being himself. Yet according to every major teacher from Jesus through Freud "to be yourself" is a great virtue.

Dali himself has never suggested that his immodesty, mendacity, technical virtuosity or his flamboyance added up to a good thing. "I spend each day," he told me once, "trying my best to be Dali."

So believable are his flights into fantasy, his technique of illusion, that his paintings could be color photographs taken by a Freudian camera in the mind. This reality once removed is probably the reason that his images of soft melting watches, of legs, arms and phalluses on crutches, of women whose torsos are chests of empty drawers, are so memorable. It is as though you have seen the pictures in your own dreams.

This fortunate habit of being able to reach into the unconscious began when Salvador was a child. Like most firstborn Spanish boys he was treated like royalty within the family circle. He was dressed in a kingly robe, a gilded crown. He carried a sceptre around the house until he found an old crutch in the attic and used that instead. During that time he actually did tip over a chest of drawers, and the drawers fell out. He lived in his own world, often hallucinating, sometimes unable to tell the real from the illusion. He carried a cut glass crystal bottle stopper and looked at the multi-imaged world through it.

Unlike many artists of his time Dali did not frequent cafes and brothels. The sex in his first affair, which began when he was 13 and lasted five years, was limited to fondling his girl's breasts and kissing her.

When Dali the virgin first arrived in Paris, he visited the famous brothels: *le Charbanis, le One Two Two,* and *le Panier Fleuri,* but though he loved the decor, he found the women ugly, fat and distasteful. He masturbated. In his dictated book *The Unspeakable Confessions of Salvador Dali,* he says: "I spent a great part of my time painting alone and naked in my bedroom, and it often happened that I would put my brush down so as to take my cock in the same hand and go from one pleasure to another, living through the same ecstasy." He painted *The Great Masturbator* around this time.

Then came Gala, the girl he loved and married, and Dali's painting and his personality changed. The "fits" that had made him suicidal became fewer and milder. "Without love, without Gala—I would no longer be Dali, that is the truth I will never stop shouting. She is my blood, my oxygen." Rarely has a marriage worked so well or lasted so long. Gala was a lover, wife, mistress, mother, model, and physician. It is doubtful that Dali ever considered sex with another woman.

In his painting, meanwhile, Dali had enjoyed an association with the Surrealists, but broke with them and their leader André Breton over the scatalogical subject matter in many of his works. The Surrealists, he wrote, would allow blood and a little shit in his paintings but not shit alone. He was "authorized to paint the sexual organs but no anal fantasies. Any anus was taken in very bad humor." He continued an individual friendship with many of the surrealists, but it soon became obvious that he did not need their support. He was well on his way to fame and fortune.

When, some day all of Dali's erotic paintings will be collected in a book, it will contain more than a thousand pages rich in variety. The erotic art of Salvador Dali delved deep into the conscious mind, dredging up other illusions, hallucinations, fantasies, and all the buried emotional treasure of human variations on love and sex. And though these erotic images conjured up by the Spanish master may at first seem to have an ephemeral quality, they do not fade easily after they are seen.

His eroticism is that of unfulfilled reality. It is not surprising that preoccupation with masturbation and so-called perversions—scatology, pederasty, cunnilingus, fellatio and all the other infinite variations—have been so tellingly disclosed in his erotic drawings and paintings.

The public, the galleries, the collectors have enjoyed, praised and purchased his works, but they are still critical of his insistence of being Dali. Dali, however, wrote of his two most important goals:

"1. To make my prison as early as possible. This has been done.
2. To become, as far as possible, something of a multimillionaire and this too has been done."

Like Masson, Salvador Dali was a Surrealist, but his visual definition of the world beyond reality differed greatly. In this spacious Dali world the lovers reveal a tragic dichotomy; the female stabs the man while at the same time she delights him through fellatio.

This erotic outdoor scene, Le Jardin des Hespérides, *was painted by the Surrealist Max Ernst. In it imaginary human-like creatures indulge in an esoteric variety of thinly-disguised sexual acts. Like Masson and Dali, Ernst was one of the seminal Surrealists.*

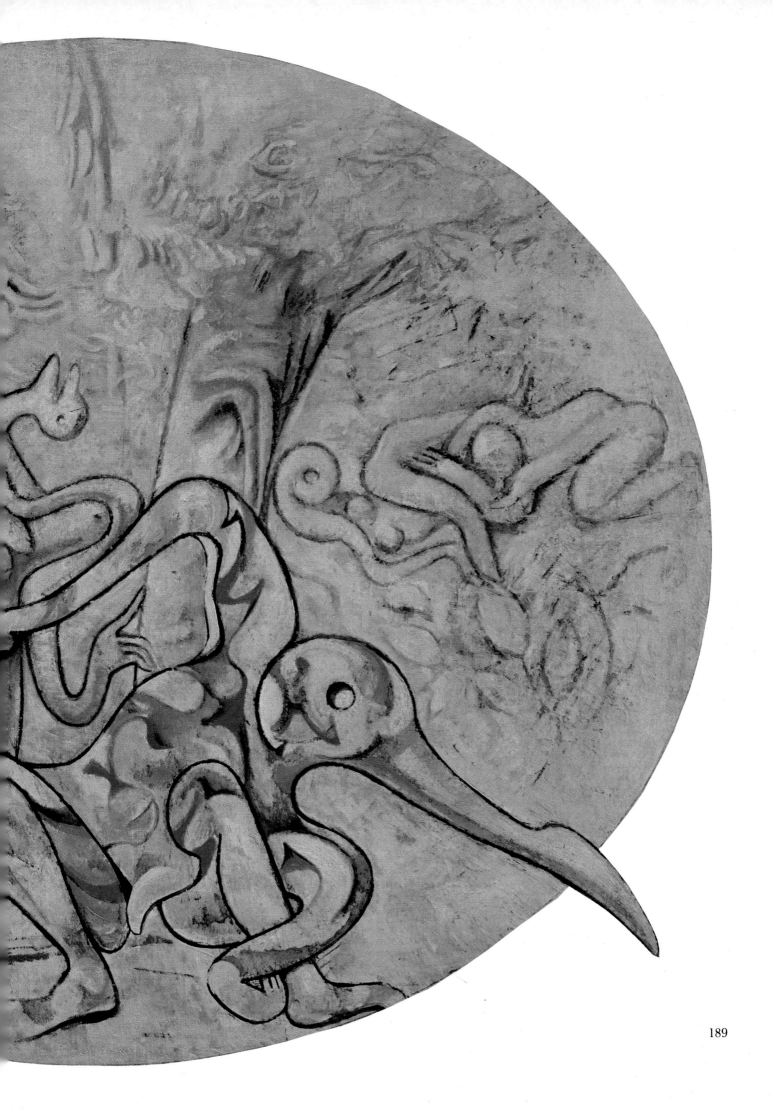

190

Under a mysterious glowing sun, Roberto Matta Echaurren has created a violent world that seems to shatter as though from an explosion. Sensuality and death dominate. Knives speed like bullets, a couple make violent love, while others continue the dance of life.

191

In Black Torso *the German painter and professor of art Paul Wunderlich has created a work of disturbing emotional emulations. He provides a strong element of mystery and suspense by the clothed-unclothed effect, with all the female erotic zones exposed.*

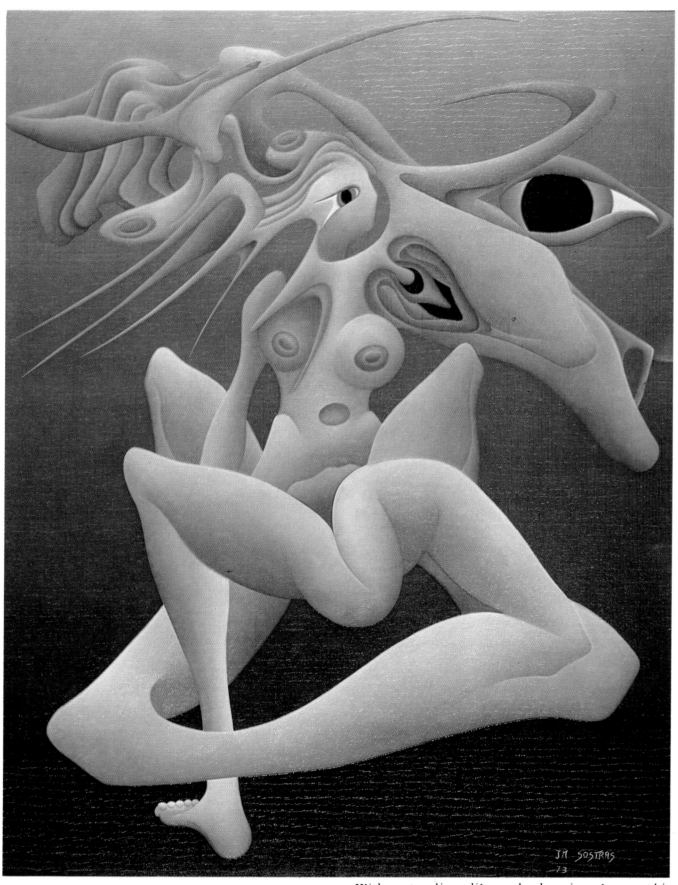

With expanding life and changing forms, this painting by Sostras, a descendant of the Surrealists, shows a strong influence from ancient India and Tibet. Tension is indicated by the extended arms and floating breasts and testicles. Note the eye of Buddha.

HANS BELLMER

Actually, Bellmer studied anatomy from every possible angle and reproduced it in depth like a three-dimensional X-ray vision. In his work one form merges into another, yet one sees where his lines go. There is no confusion as one arm, leg, breast melts into another. Bellmer's humor is often black, but occasionally a light side comes through as in the painting, opposite, of female legs and torso.

He combines breasts, vulva, mouth, anus, navel in logically interchangeable form, but the viewer can see the whole at once even if some anatomical parts are moved about or missing. As Bellmer once wrote, "The body is like a sentence which invites dissection so that its true meaning may be reconstituted in an endless series of anagrams." Some of his works have been called anatomical anagrams, puzzles in which we can find new and different meanings. He believed that the whole body made up the world of the senses, that the imagination is seeded not only in the brain but in the body. Just as Lawrence believed that the impulses, the race memory, the instincts were in the blood, so Bellmer went further, to postulate that the whole body, muscles, genitals, sinews, guts, all in their various manifestations and motions, contributed to ideas and imagination. "Mathematics," he wrote, "was not invented by the head alone."

Bellmer believed in desire as the root of all life— "Desire precedes being." Again like Miller and Lawrence, he swam against the current towards freedom for people to express themselves fully. Though he emphasized sensuality, he approached his work like a physiologist as well as a visual poet.

He was critical of sexual taboos as inventions of man which are not natural to the functioning of the human body. Most of us would agree with his statement, "The origin of that part of my work that scandalizes is the fact that for me the world is a scandal."

Hans Bellmer's father was a tyrannical policeman in the household, authoritarian, an early member of the Nazi party. Young Hans once concocted a story of a Jewish ancestor and the distraught Aryan father spent months furtively trying to trace the imaginary, unworthy forebear. Fortunately for us, Bellmer also reacted to his parentage in more productive ways. Thanks no doubt to the influence of his warm and generous mother, he has left hundreds of drawings and paintings, all meticulously executed, of which many depict men being used by women, others reveal the artist's belief in desire and sensuality.

Though he had his own advertising agency, Bellmer left Nazi Germany for Paris in 1938, when he was thirty-six. He had a strange avocation: he had discovered some dolls in his mother's effects and at about the same time seen *The Tales of Hoffman,* in which a doll comes to life. His published theories about the evolution of dolls and the doll as a fetish appealed to the Surrealists in Paris, and he lived and worked there until the city fell to the Germans. He narrowly escaped death as an "idle Jew," and spent the war years in the south of France.

Just as the work of Henry Miller was influenced by the painting of George Grosz, so was that of Hans Bellmer. Grosz advised him for a time and was astonished at the superior draftmanship of his short-time protégé. As Henry Miller dissected the human body in text, Bellmer dissected it in drawings. Some of his descriptions sound like Miller's prose. "Greasy eyelets floating on broth, sunken bulbous tangles, twisted tresses of muscular tissues, networks of bone and teeth, intestinal-like coils of the brain, petrified safety matches, masses of rectangular cells, open filigree work, crystalized splinters, reminiscent of a cutlass grinding stone at sunset."

This is a lithograph of the last painting of Hans Bellmer, master of erotic form and substance. A Surrealist, Bellmer, in his paintings, collages, lithographs, and dolls dealt with sexual appetites. His women were beautiful and passionate. The title is The Striped Stockings.

(Overleaf) In one of the masterpieces of erotic art, Hans Bellmer has painted a double portrait of himself and a beautiful woman, drawing his head just above the vulva. The work is a collage that includes pearls, lace, and crumpled paper on pen and ink and paint.

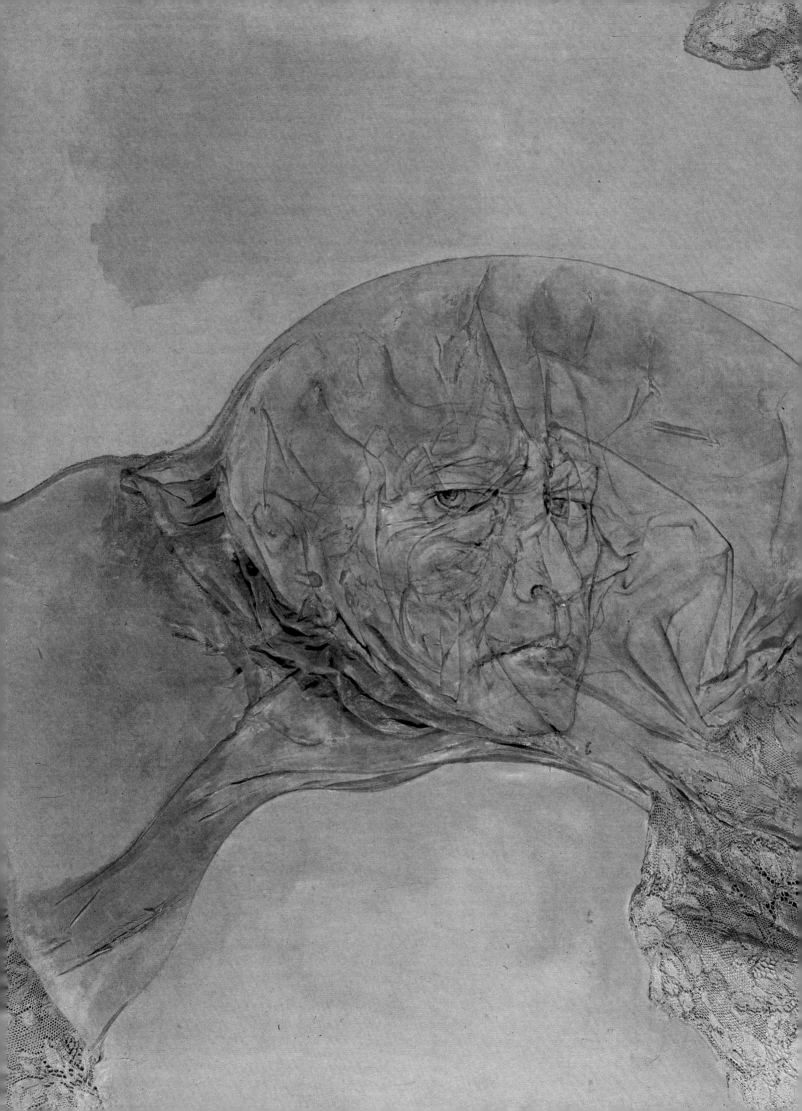

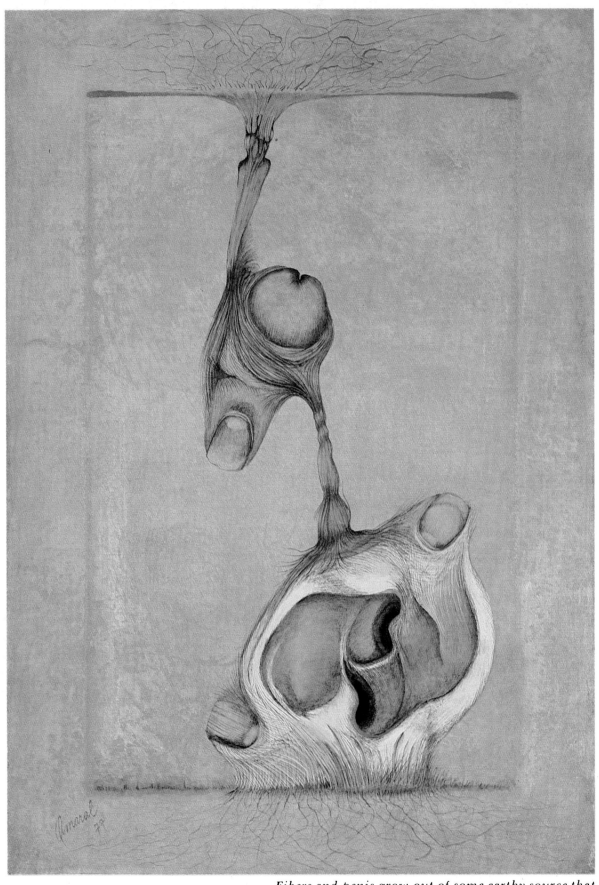

Fibers and penis grow out of some earthy source that reaches out for roots in the sky. By joining the penis and finger together the artist gives a hint of masturbation. Amaral, the California-born artist, titled this unique work Plant Rooted at Both Ends.

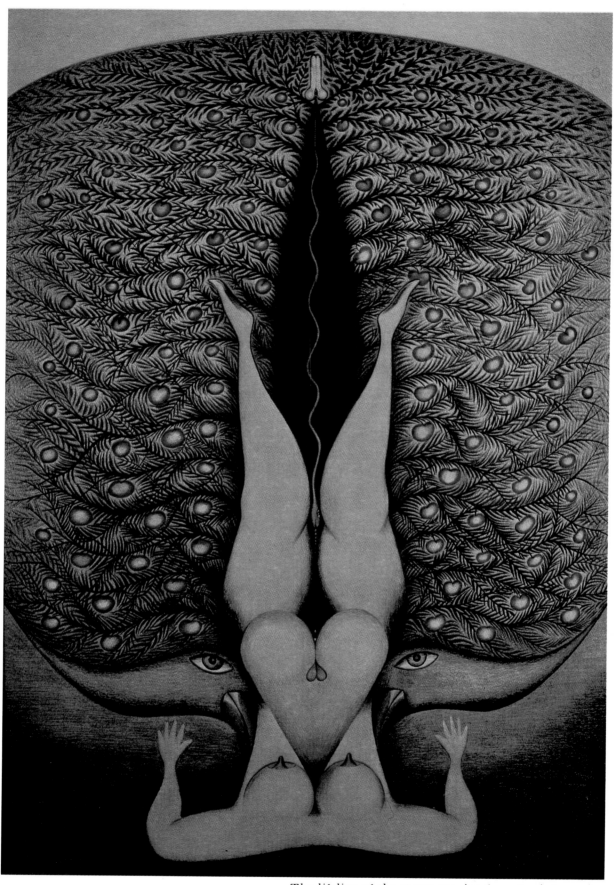

The lifeline of the sperm moving from penis to vagina forms the center of this work by Friedrich Schröder-Sonnenstern. The peacock motif, buttocks shaped as a heart, and the pointed breasts complete this erotic vision, while moving the eye and the mind well beyond reality.

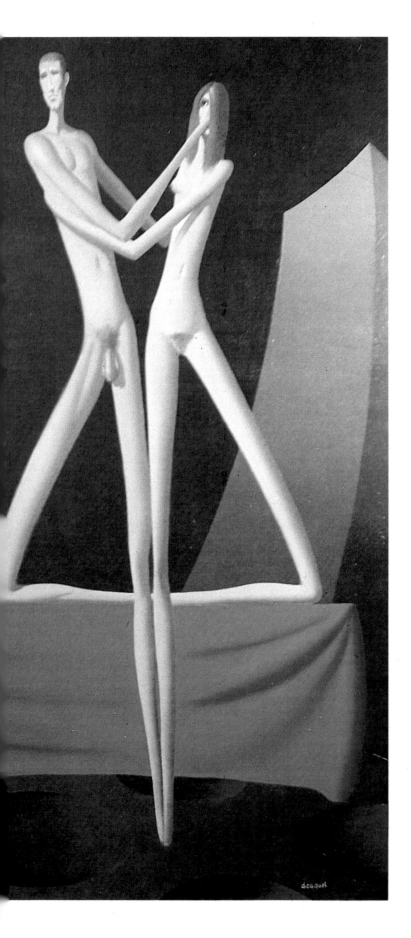

In an original use of space Gérard Deuquet in Les Couples *illustrates the continuing problem of the eternal triangle pointed up by the leg pattern of the man and woman located on the right. The height of the participants is greatly exaggerated by the background.*

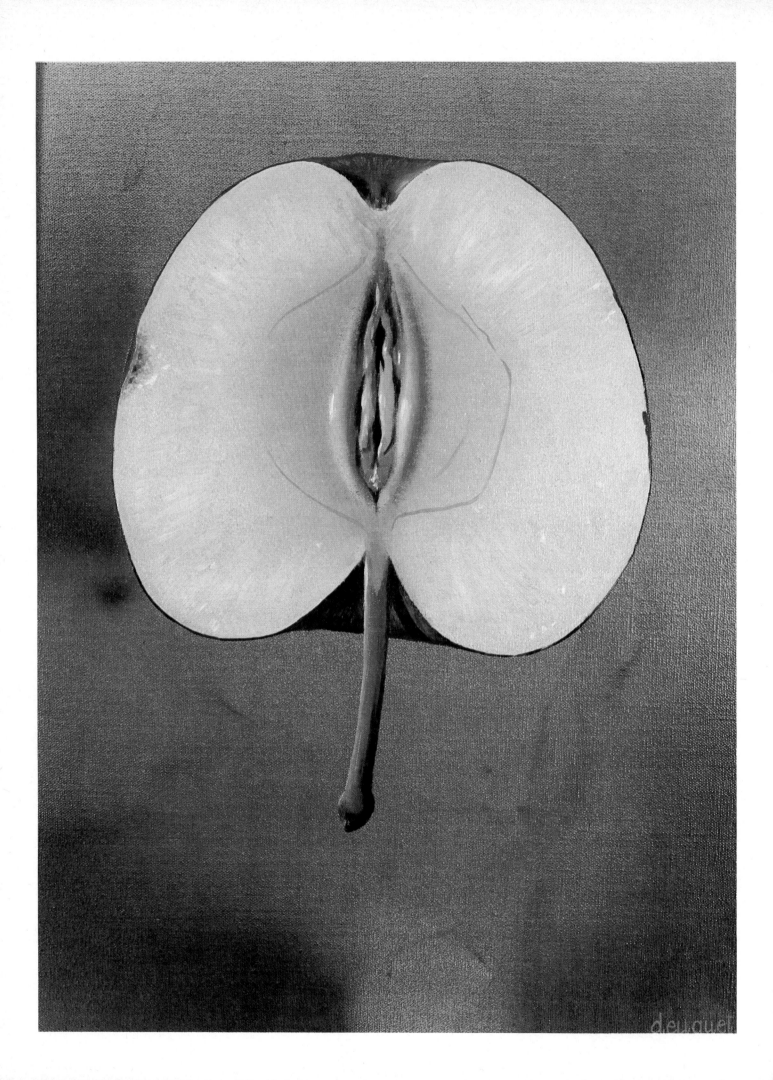

Above is an apple represented as a symbol of the female sex as painted by the German artist Manfred Marburger and titled Apple II. *At left is another apple, painted as a female symbol by the French artist Gérard Deuquet and called* The Apple of Adam.

(Overleaf) Evocative of the later Cubist artists is this work titled Nude on the Table. *Painted by Stehli, it shows how Cubist technique was incorporated into more realistic concepts. The style and overhead perspective indicate it was painted around mid-century.*

206

Health and Strength II *is the storytelling title of the German painter Volker Stoecks' modern treatment of a very muscular male in motion. Using the principal of the repetitive stroboscopic flash, Stoecks has refined and added depth to the concept of freezing movement.*

In a wholly invented world peopled by strange anthropomorphic types, the émigré Russian painter Mihail Chemiakin, now Paris-based, has represented Harlequin with a nose like an erotic Pinocchio. Political and social currents underlie his work.

Males and females appear interchangeable in this sexual sequence painted by Mexico's Francisco Toledo, titled La Ronda. *Birds and animals dominate Toledo's erotic themes (pages 64-65). The bird represents the male symbol and is depicted sucking at the female breast.*

Richard Lindner's The Couple, *painted in 1961, has a simple heterosexual theme that becomes erotic through the use of flowing lines and its vivid colors. The sexuality lies as much in what is invisible as that which, like the woman's breasts, is exposed.*

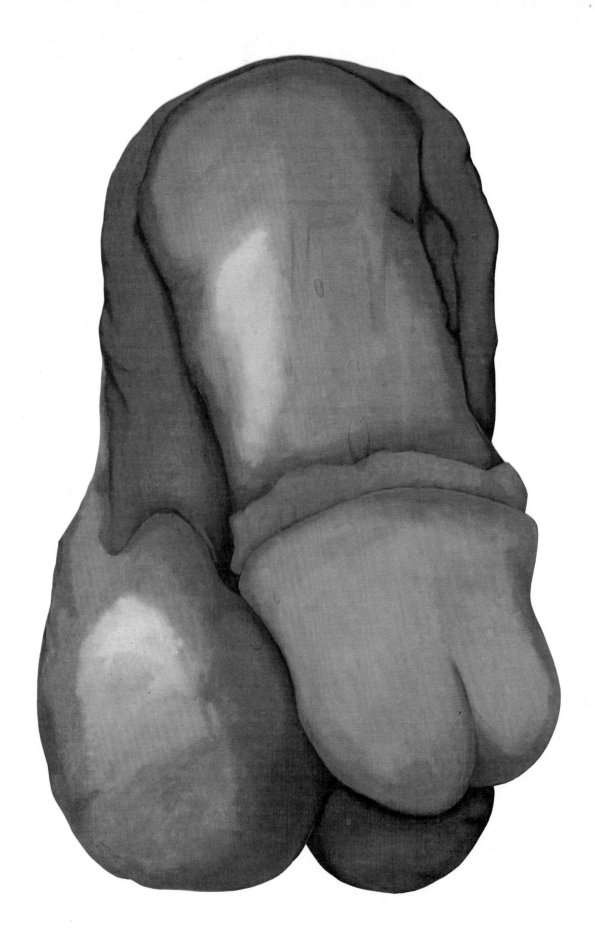

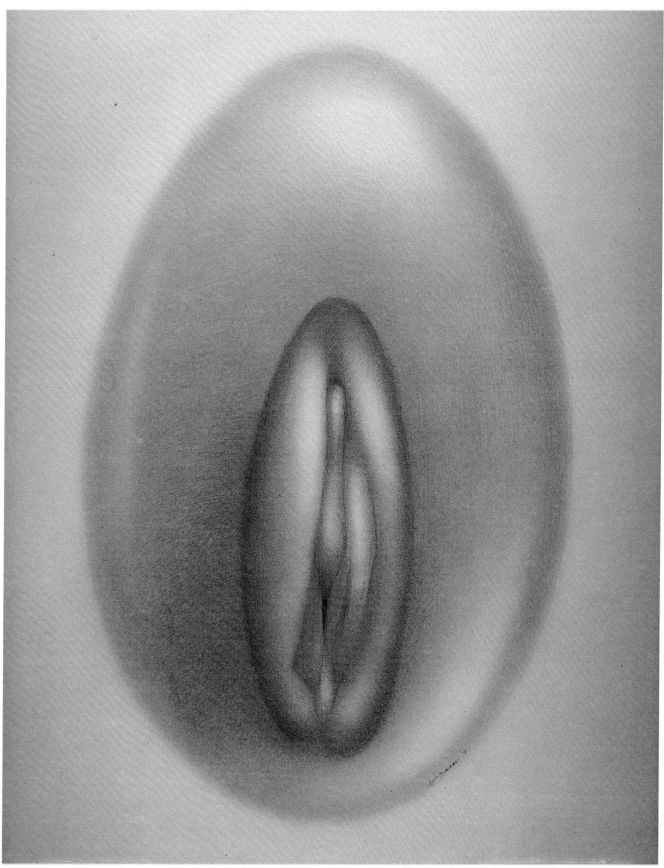

There is a humorous and very human quality in the way Richard Oliver has painted this untitled symbol of male sexuality. Unlike many macho images that show the penis as a threatening weapon, Oliver's concept is of a benign and safe, friendly teddy bear.

Erotic yet almost abstract is this visualization of the female sexual symbol. The artist Igor Medvedev-Mead has made a modern votive offering in the form of the essence of woman's sexuality. The title is Bindu-Yoni, which is vulva in the Hindu language.

A hand spreads the legs, exposing the vulva in this bronze cast fragment of a woman's torso by the internationally acclaimed sculptor George Segal. The work is called Delta of Venus—*which happens also to be the title of the erotic book by Anaïs Nin.*

212

Acknowledgments

My *special* thanks to my wife, Elisabeth Girard Smith, whose ability, energy, interest, and affection have been indispensable. Cheers!

A book is never created without the assistance of interested and interesting people, and TWENTIETH CENTURY MASTERS OF EROTIC ART is no exception. I wish to gratefully acknowledge the cooperation of several friends without whose assistance and counsel this work would not have been possible: Dr. J.-M. Lo Duca, distinguished publisher and editor in Paris; Booton Herndon, author and editor; Philip A. Bruno, of the Staempfli Gallery in New York; Saki Karavas, José Hernandez and Sharon Smith Hernandez, Harvey Shuster, Leonard Slater, and Walasse Ting.

My thanks to the following friends and colleagues around the world who have given encouragement, advice and assistance:

IN THE USA: Henry Miller, Leo Castelli, Louise Deutschman, Alex Rosenberg, Paul Jenkins, Jacques Kaplan, Dr. Paul Mocsanyi, Hugh Hefner, Teressa Rice, Sidney and Carroll Janis, Gene Basin, José Tasende, Dr. Vance Kondon, Mary Moore Little, Carole Ann Klonarides, Irving Karp, Carlos La Manya, John Boone, Kenneth Quail, Christopher Dark, Jean Kauth, Lori Ciancaglini, Françoise Gilot Salk, Bonnie Herndon, Don Brewer, the University of California at San Diego Library: Rare Book Department and Research Department, San Diego Public Library Research Department, and San Diego Museum of Art Library.

IN CANADA: Teresa Bjornson.

IN ENGLAND: Victor A. Lownes, Graham Ovenden, Louis de Wet, Wolfgang Fisher, Simon Wilson, Peyton Skipwith, and Barry Miller.

IN FRANCE: André-François Petit, Jean Luc and Kathy de Carbuccia, Eugène Braun-Munk, Octave Negru, the late M. d'Halluin, Isy Brachot, and Jacqueline Passever.

IN SWITZERLAND: Gérald Nordman and Oscar Ghez.

IN SPAIN: Salvador Dali, Pablo Runyon Kelting, Gloria Kirby, Rosa Maria Subirana and the staff of the Museo Picasso.

IN VIENNA: Dr. Ernst Fuchs.

IN JAPAN: Raymond Bushell, Misagi Ashida, Kazuo Suzuki, Muneyoshi Kaigo, Eric Sackheim, Masuo Ikeda, Hiroshi Aiko, Masatake Maruyama, and Ryuichi Fujii.

I am equally grateful to all the artists, collectors, and museums that have kindly allowed me to reproduce their works. Their names and their gallery and museum affiliations will be found listed under Works of Art beginning on page 216.

Bibliography

Ajit, Mookerjee. *Tantra Art*. New Delhi: Kumar Gallery, 1966.

Arnheim, Rudolf. *Art and Visual Perception*. Berkeley: University of California Press, 1969.

Bernard Louedin. Bibliophilic edition, 1977.

Boas, George and Harold Holmes Wrenn. *What Is A Picture?* New York: Shocken Books, 1966.

Brown, Frederick. *An Impersonation of Angels—A Biography of Jean Cocteau*. New York: Viking Press, 1968.

Campagne, Jean-Marc. *Alfred Courmes,* Paris: Editions Eric Losfeld, 1973.

Catalogue de l'oeuvre peinte de Labisse, 1927-79. Preface by Jean Cassou. Brussels: Editions Isy Brachot, 1979.

Chang, Jolan. *The Tao of Love and Sex*. New York: E.P. Dutton, 1977.

Chemiakin, Mihail. *Dessins*. Paris: Galerie J.C. Gaubert, 1975.

Compton, Michael. *Pop Art*. London: Hamlyn Publishing Group, 1970.

Daix, Pierre. *Picasso*. New York: Praeger Publishers, 1965.

Dali, Salvador, *Diary of a Genius*. New York: Doubleday and Company, Inc., 1965.

Dali, Salvador. *The Unspeakable Confessions of Salvador Dali*. New York: William Morrow and Company, Inc., 1976.

Davies, Margaret. *Apollinaire*. New York: St. Martins Press, 1964.

d'Harnoncourt, Anne and Kynaston McShine (eds.). *Marcel Duchamp*. New York: The Museum of Modern Art, 1973.

Eros, Spring Vol. 1, #1, 1962.

Erotic Art. New York: The New School of Art Center, 1973.

Faulkner, William. *Sanctuary* and *Requiem for a Nun*. New York: New American Library, 1961.

Fille de Joie, New York: Grove Press, 1967.

Franc, Helen M. *An Introduction To See*. New York: Museum of Modern Art, 1973.

Friday, Nancy. *Men In Love*. New York: Delacorte Press, 1980.

Gautier, Théophile. *Mademoiselle de Maupin*. The Pierre Louys Society, 1927.

Giacomo Manzù. La Jolla: Tasende Gallery, 1979.

Gimpel, René. *Diary of an Art Dealer*. New York: Farrar, Straus, and Giroux, 1966.

Girodias, Maurice. *The Olympia Reader*. New York: Ballentine Books, 1970.

Haftmann, Werner. *Painting in the Twentieth Century*. New York: Praeger Publishers, 1971.

Hammond, Paul. *French Undressing*. London: Jupiter Books, 1976.

Hans Bellmer. Paris: Editions Filipacchi, 1971.

Holloway, Emory (ed.). *The Collected Poems of Walt Whitman*. New York: The Book League of America, 1942.

Hunt, Morton. *Sexual Behavoir in the 1970s*. Playboy Press, 1974.

Ikeda, Masuo. *Mixed Fruit*. Lithographs and Poems. Tokyo: Nantenshi Gallery, 1977.

Illing, Richard. *Japanese Erotic Art and the Life of the Courtesan*. New York: St Martins Press, 1979.

José Luis Cuevas. La Jolla: Tasende Gallery, 1979.

Jung, Carl G. (ed.). *Man and His Symbols*. New York: Dell Publishing Co., 1964.

Kultermann, Udo. *New Realism*. Greenwich: New York Graphic Society, 1972.

"Lawrence's Manuscript of Fantasia of the Unconscious," Berkeley: University of California Bancroftiana, No. 74, Feb., 1980.

Lo Duca, J.-M. *Histoire de l'Erotisme*. Paris: Editions Pygmalion, 1980.

Lucie-Smith, Edward. *Eroticism in Western Art*. London: Thames and Hudson, Ltd., 1972.

Mackworth, Cecily. *Guillaume Apollinaire and the Cubist Life*. New York: Horizon Press, 1963.

Malamud, Bernard. *Dubin's Lives*. New York: Avon Books, 1980.

Masuo Ikeda. Bibliophilic edition. Bitjutsu Shuppan-sha, 1978.

Miller, Henry. *My Life and Times*. La Jolla: Gemini Smith, Inc., 1971.

Miller, Henry. *To Paint Is To Love Again*. New York: Grossman Publishers, 1968.

Moran, James Sterling. *The Classic Woman.* La Jolla: Gemini Smith, Inc., 1973.

Outsiders. Arts Council of Great Britain, 1979.

Nabokov, Vladimir. *Lolita.* New York: Crest Books, 1959.

Phaidon Dictionary of Twentieth Century Art. London: Phaidon Press, Ltd., 1973.

Rawson, Philip. *Erotic Art of the East.* New York: Prometheus Press, 1968.

Rodman, Selden (ed.). *100 Modern Poems.* New York: New American Library, 1958.

Rubin, William. *Dada, Surrealism, and Their Heritage.* New York: The Museum of Modern Art.

Rubin, William and Carolyn Larchner. *André* Masson. New York: The Museum of Modern Art, 1976.

Sensuous Sculpture. New York: Alex Rosenberg Gallery, 1979.

Smith, Bradley. *The American Way of Sex.* La Jolla: Gemini Smith, Inc., 1978.

Smith, Bradley. *Erotic Art of the Masters: The 18th, 19th & 20th Centuries.* La Jolla: Gemini Smith, Inc., 1976.

Smith, T.R. (ed.). *Poetica Erotica.* New York: Horace Liveright, Inc., 1931.

Solier, René de. *Jane Graverol.* Brussels: Editions André de Rache, 1974.

Sypher, Wylie (ed.). *Art History: An Anthology of Modern Criticism.* New York: Vintage Books, 1963.

Ting, Walasse. *Red Mouth.* Bibliophilic edition, 1977.

Waldberg, Patrick. *Eros Modern Style.* Paris: J.J. Pauvert, 1964.

Warhol, Andy. *Andy Warhol's Index Book.* New York: Random House, 1967.

Warhol, Andy. *Blue Movie.* New York: Grove Press, 1970.

Webb, Peter. *The Erotic Arts.* London: Secker & Warburg, 1975.

Zimmer. *Myths and Symbols in Indian Art and Civilization.* Pantheon Books., Inc., 1946.

Index

The Works of Art

24 William Copley, *Midnight Cowboy*, 1972, acrylic, 114.3 x 147.3 cm. Collection of the artist, New York.

25 Copley, *I am Curious*, 1973, acrylic, 162.6 x 132 cm. Collection of the artist, New York.

26-27 Alexander Calder, *Gouache #606*, 1967, 74.3 x 109.9 cm. Estate of Alexander Calder; Courtesy M. Knoedler & Co., Inc., New York.

28-29 Otto Dix, *Sailor With Black Prostitute*, 1922, watercolor, 50.8 x 38.7 cm. Collection of Vance E. Kondon, La Jolla, California.

31 Henry Miller, *D'aprés Schatz (After Schatz)*, 1973, lithograph, 48.5 x 30.5 cm. Collection of Bradley Smith.

32-33 John Altoon, *F-29 (Man with Whip; Women Tied)*, 1966, pen, ink and airbrush, 76.2 x 101.6 cm. Tibor de Nagy Gallery, New York.

34-35 Richard Merkin, *Charvet et Fils*, 1975, tempera, 122 x 183 cm. Terry Dintenfass Gallery, New York.

36-37 Merkin, *The House of Two Mysterious Blondes in Their Early Twenties*, 1975, tempera, 122 x 183 cm. Collection of the artist, New York.

38 Fritz Scholder, *Macho Woman*, 1977, oil, 101.6 x 76.2 cm. Collection of the artist, Scottsdale, Arizona.

39 Walasse Ting, *Tiger Man*, 1972, collage on paper, 183 x 152.4 cm. Lefebre Gallery, New York.

40 George Grosz, untitled, 1920-21, watercolor, 67.3 x 25 cm. Collection of Victor Lownes, London.

41 Giacomo Manzú, *Generale Tedesco*, 1941, ink on paper, 33.7 x 16.5 cm. Tasende Gallery, La Jolla, California.

42-43 Angela Gorgus, untitled series of gouaches, 1978-79, 20.3 x 25.4 cm each. Collection of Victor Lownes, London.

44 Masuo Ikeda, untitled watercolors from special limited edition of *Mixed Fruit*, (above) 1977, (below) 1976, 17.5 x 27 cm each. Nantenshi Gallery, Tokyo; Bancho Gallery, Tokyo; Staempfli Gallery, New York.

45 Ikeda, *Joryu-gaka no Danna (Husband of the Painter)*, 1978, watercolor. Nantenshi Gallery, Tokyo; Bancho Gallery, Tokyo; Staempfli Gallery, New York.

46-47 Clifton Karhu, *Don't Forget Self Reflection; It's Good to Expand Your Good Points; Go Slowly and You Can Enjoy the Scenery; Legs Are Precious Too*, 1979, detail, watercolor, scroll. Courtesy of the artist, Kyoto.

48-49 Larry Rivers, *Japanese Erotic Art*, 1974, pencil and colored pencil, 149.9 x 213.4 cm. Collection of the artist, New York.

Fantasy

51 Ljuba, *Sabra ou Hommage à Mme Roben (Sabra or Hommage to Mrs. Roben)*, 1972, oil, 195 x 130 cm. Galerie de Seine, Paris.

53 Oleg Tselkov, *Two Personae*, 1979, oil, 238.8 x 193 cm. Eduard Nakhamkin Fine Arts, Inc., New York.

54-55 Clovis Trouille, *Le Magicien*, 1944, oil, 127 x 154.9 cm. Courtesy J.M. Lo Duca, Paris.

56 Mitsuyoshi Haruguchi, *Tamashii No Rinne (Transmigration of Souls)*, 1978, tempera on board, 130 x 130 cm. Osaka Forme Gallery, Tokyo.

57 Haruguchi, *Tori Sugiru Uma (Horse Passing)*, 1973, tempera on board, 90.9 x 90.9 cm. Osaka Forme Gallery, Tokyo.

58 Graham Ovenden, *The Old Garden*, 1975-78, oil, 91.4 x 132.1 cm. Private

collection.

59 Pamela Mower-Conner, *Lori Jane at 13*, acrylic on masonite, 1976, 76.2 x 101.6 cm. Collector's Choice Gallery, Laguna Beach, California.

60-61 Ljuba, *Le Cri (The Scream)*, 1976, oil, 130 x 162 cm. Galerie de Seine, Paris.

62-63 José de Creeft, *Odalisque*, 1940, tempera, 15.2 x 30.5 cm. Kennedy Galleries, Inc., New York.

64-65 Francisco Toledo, *Lady Serving the Lion*, 1965, pencil, ink and watercolor, 49.5 x 66 cm. Mary Moore Gallery, La Jolla, CA.

66 Martha Edelheit, *Female Flesh Wall*, 1964-65, oil, 203.2 x 495.3 cm. Collection of the artist, New York.

67 Clara Tice, untitled illustration for privately printed edition of *Mademoiselle de Maupin*, by Théophile Gautier, watercolor and etching, 14.9 x 11.1 cm. Collection of Bradley Smith.

68 Horst Janssen, *Vriederich*, 1978, watercolor, 28 x 60.5 cm. Galerie Brockstedt, Hamburg.

69 José Luis Cuevas, *Pareja #3*, 1976, watercolor, 24.8 x 31.8 cm. Tasende Gallery, La Jolla, CA.

70-71 H.R. Giger, *Paysage XV, Bomarzo*, 1972-73, acrylic on paper, 70 x 100 cm. Collection of the artist, Zurich.

72 Pino Zac, *Aspiration*, 1978, oil, 95 x 95 cm. Courtesy J.-M. Lo Duca, Paris.

73 Zac, *Un Large Sourire (A Broad Smile)*, 1978, oil, 95 x 95 cm. Courtesy J.-M. Lo Duca, Paris.

74-75 Roland Bourigeaud, *Le Divan de Babylone (The Couch of Babylon)*, 1966, oil, 150 x 194 cm. Courtesy J.-M. Lo Duca, Paris; Private Collection, Tokyo.

76 Lucien Coutaud, untitled, oil, Musée National d'Art Moderne, Paris.

77 Andrès Cillero, *Condestable*, 1970, mixed media, 94 x 80 x 7 cm. Courtesy of the artist, Madrid; Collection of Juan Ignacio de Blas, Madrid.

78-79 Carlos Revilla, *Le Bleu du Ciel (Blue Sky)*, 1973, oil, 100 x 120 cm. Galerie André François Petit, Paris.

(right) Revilla, *Le Silence*, detail, 1974, oil, 100 x 100 cm. Galerie André-François Petit.

80 Henk Pander, untitled, 1971, watercolor, 53.3 x 73 cm. Collection of the artist, Portland, Oregon.

81 Pander, *Erotic Scene Over Holland*, 1979, oil, 137.2 x 162.6 cm. Private Collection.

Romance

83 Elias Friedensohn, *The Rape of Europa*, 1973, oil, 50.8 x 40.6 cm. Terry Dintenfass Gallery, New York.

84-85 Ryonosuke Fukui, *Ai (Love)*, 1970, oil, 90.9 x 116.7 cm. Fujii Gallery, Tokyo.

86 Tadashi Ishimoto, *Higata (Beach at Ebb Tide)*, 1976, iwaenogu (watercolor), 170 x 92 cm. Courtesy of Gallery Saikodo, Tokyo.

87 Ishimoto, *Amaoto (Sound of Rain)*, 1979, iwaenogu (watercolor), 80 x 96 cm. Gallery Saikodo, Tokyo.

88 D.H. Lawrence, *Dance Sketch*, 1928 oil, 38.1 x 43.2 cm. Collection of Saki Karavas, Taos, New Mexico.

89 Lawrence, *Fight with an Amazon*, 1926-27, oil, 73.6 x 99 cm. Collection of Saki Karavas, Taos, New Mexico.

90-91 Ernst Fuchs, *Liebestraumverknotung (Tangled Dream of Love)*, 1965, gouache, 37 x 52 cm. Courtesy of the artist, Vienna.

92 Fuchs, *Die Rast der Ballerina (The Rest of a Ballerina)*, 1970, pastel on canvas, 100 x 100 cm. Courtesy of the artist, Vienna.

93 Fuchs, *Die Rose (The Rose)*, 1966, gouache, 48 x 32 cm. Courtesy of the artist, Vienna.

94 Egon Schiele, *Two Women*, 1911, watercolor, 38 x 28 cm. Fischer Fine Art Ltd., London.

95 Schiele, *Lovers*, 1911, tempera, watercolor and pencil, 48.3 x 30.5 cm. Fischer Fine Art Ltd., London.

96 Giacomo Manzù, *Pittore con modella (Painter with model)*, 1943, pastel and tempera, 70.5 x 50.2 cm. Tasende Gallery, La Jolla, California.

97 Auguste Chabaud, *Isorel au Salon (Isorel in the Drawing Room)*, 1905, oil, 106 x 76 cm. Musée du Petit Palais, Geneva.

98-99 Paul Delvaux, *Les Femmes Tumultueuses (Effervescent Women)*, 1968, gouache, 72 x 106 cm. Galerie Isy Brachot, Brussels, Paris.

100 Paul Wunderlich, *Polar Bear Rug*, 1971, drawing and watercolor, 66 x 82.6 cm. Staempfli Gallery, New York.

101 Wunderlich, untitled, 1978, pencil, watercolor and oil, 86 x 73 cm. Galerie Negru, Paris.

102 Hans Moller, *Torso*, 1978, watercolor, 61 x 45.7 cm. Collection of Mrs. Hans Moller, Allentown, Pennsylvania.

103 Charles Demuth, *Turkish Bath Scene with Self Portrait*, 1918, watercolor, 27.9 x 21.6 cm. Kennedy Galleries, Inc., New York.

104-105 Bernard Louedin, *Le Royaume Millénaire (The Thousand Year Old Kingdom)*, 1979, oil, 83.8 x 104.1 cm. Collection of the artist.

105 Egon Schiele, *Two Loving Women*, 1913, pencil and gouache on paper, 33 x 49 cm.

Collection of Vance E. Kondon, La Jolla, California.

106 Ljubomir Milinkov, *La Ronde des Moutons (The Sheep Round About)*, oil, 24.5 x 19 cm. Collection of Bradley Smith.

107 Johannes Grützke, *Glück und Mühen (Happiness and Efforts)*, 1976, oil, 205 x 180 cm. Galerie Godula Buchholz K.G., Munich.

108-109 Pablo Picasso, *Dos Figuras y un Gato (Two Figures and a Cat)*, 1901-02, pencil and watercolor, 18 x 26.5 cm. Museo Picasso, Barcelona. © S.P.A.D.E.M., Paris; V.A.G.A., New York.

110 Leonor Fini, *Extase Blonde (Blonde Ecstasy)*, 1968, oil. Courtesy J.-M. Lo Duca, Paris.

111 Félix Labisse, *Le Petit Ventre (Torso)*, 1938, oil, 50 x 40 cm. Courtesy J.-M. Lo Duca, Paris; Galerie Isy Brachot, Brussels, Paris.

112-113 Jean Paul Cleren, *Le Rêve (The Dream)*, 1970, oil, 165 x 235 cm. Courtesy J.-M. Lo Duca, Paris; Galerie Lambert Monet, Geneva.

114 Karolus Lodenkämper, *Doppelbild Olympia I (Double Image Olympia I)*, 1971, oil, 100 x 80 cm. Galerie Negru, Paris.

115 Henk Pander, *Terri and Victoria*, 1978, watercolor, 74.9 x 111.8 cm. Collection of the artist, Portland, Oregon.

116-117 Fernando Botero, *Les Amants (The Lovers)*, 1973, oil, 181 x 191 cm. John Berggruen Gallery, San Francisco.

Symbols

119 Paul Delvaux, *Chrysis*, 1967, oil, 160 x 140 cm. Courtesy J.-M. Lo Duca, Paris; Galerie Isy Brachot, Brussels, Paris.

121 Lamberto Camerini, *Innocenza (Innocence)*, 1975, oil, 60 x 79 cm. Courtesy J.-M. Lo Duca, Paris; Private Collection, Turin.

122 Louis de Wet, *Harpy*, oil and egg emulsion. Courtesy of the artist.

123 Alessandri, *Eve et le Serpent*, 1965, oil, 122 x 200 cm. Courtesy of Lorenzo Alessandri and of J.-M. Lo Duca, Paris.

124 Robert Rauschenberg, *Gulf*, 1969, lithograph, 106.7 x 76.2 cm. © U.L.A.E. Castelli Graphics, New York.

125 Robert Beauchamp, *Giant*, 1975, oil on paper, 56 x 76 cm. Collection of the artist.

126-127 Beauchamp, *Witches' Sabbath*, 1961, oil on paper on panel, 22.2 x 29.2 cm. Collection of Philip A. Bruno, New York.

128 Jane Graverol, *La Chute de Babylone (The Fall of Babylon)*, 1967, painting, collage on panel, 93 x 72 cm. Courtesy J.-M. Lo Duca, Paris; Private collection, Solley, Indiana.

129 Elias Friedensohn, *Gather Ye Rosebuds*, 1970, oil, 152.4 x 127 cm. Terry Dintenfass Gallery, New York.

130 Roland Bourigeaud, *La Fille de la Comtesse de Ségur (The Daughter of the Countess of Segur)*, 1969, oil, 160 x 130 cm. Courtesy, J.-M. Lo Duca, Paris; Collection of Dr. Gérard Zwang, Vaux-le-Pénil, France.

131 Jo Manning Heard, *Interlude*, 1980, oil, 101.6 x 76.2 cm. Collection of the artist, El Centro, California.

132-133 Mel Ramos, *Bananasplit*, 1970, oil, 135 x 153 cm. Collection of Bruno Bischofberger, Zurich.

134 Eberhard Schlotter, *Nocturno*, 1977, oil, 120 x 66 cm. Collection of the artist, Altea, Spain.

135 Schlotter, *Eva*, 1977, oil, 100 x 72 cm. Collection of the artist, Altea, Spain.

136 Karolus Lodenkämper, *L'Obstacle I*, 1974, oil, 200 x 200 cm. Galerie Negru, Paris.

137 Bona (Mme André Pieyre de Mandiargues), *La Double Caresse* (detail), 1979, oil on wood, 65 x 40 cm. Courtesy J.-M. Lo Duca; Collection of Sylvia Bourdon, Paris.

138-139 Klaus Liebig, *Papillon (Butterfly)*, 1975, oil, 140 x 180 cm. Galerie Godula Buchholz K.G. Munich.

140-141 Henk Pander, *Victoria and Wizard*, 1978, oil, 162.6 x 137.2 cm. Collection of the artist, Portland, Oregon.

142 Alfred Courmes, *Le Sphinx Acétylène*, 1945, oil on wood, 65 x 98 cm. Courtesy J.-M. Lo Duca, Collection of Roux.

143 Richard Lindner, *Eve*, 1969, watercolor, 107.5 x 71.5 cm. Collection of Jaques Kaplan, New York.

144 Lindner, untitled, 1950, oil, 101.5 x 56 cm. Collection of Jacques Kaplan, New York.

145 Tsugouharu Foujita, *La Dompteuse et le Lion (The Tamer and the Lion)*, 1930, oil, 147 x 91 cm. Musée du Petit Palais, Geneva.

146 Erró, *Les Merveilles de la Nature (The Wonders of Nature)*, 1978, oil on wood, 130 x 81 cm. Courtesy J.-M. Lo Duca, Paris; Galerie Sylvia Bourdon, Paris.

147 Erró, *Fantasmes*, 1979, oil on wood, 162 x 97 cm. Courtesy J.-M. Lo Duca, Paris.

The New Realism

149 John Kacere, *M. Dorman*, 1977, oil, 147.3 x 111.8 cm. O.K. Harris Works of Art, New York.

150 Hilo Chen, *Beach 52*, oil, 76.8 x 102.2 cm. Louis K. Meisel Gallery, New York.

151 Senén Ubiña, *Two Centers*, 1976, acrylic and ink, 76.2 x 50.8 cm. Collection of the artist, New York.

152 Alain Drarig, *Water Lily*, 1976, mixed media, 30.5 x 45.7 cm. Private Collection.

153 Mel Ramos, *Marquet's Mannequin*, 1979, watercolor, 77.5 x 57.2 cm. Louis K. Meisel Gallery, New York.

154-155 Hilo Chen, *Bedroom 4*, 1976, ink, 68.6 x 101.6 cm. Louis K. Meisel Gallery, New York.

156-157 Chen, *Bathroom 8*, 1976, oil, 91.4 x 32.4 cm. Louis K. Meisel Gallery, New York.

158 Igor Medvedev/Mead, *Love Goddess*, 1972, mixed media, 101.6 x 76.2 cm. Collection of Robert da Costa; Courtesy of the artist, Palo Alto, California.

159 Medvedev/Mead, *Yoni* series, 1972, mixed media, 101.6 x 76.2 cm each. Collection of the artist, Palo Alto, California.

160-161 Tom Wesselmann, *Carol Nude*, 1977, oil, 262.9 x 334.3 cm. Private Collection; Photo courtesy Sidney Janis Gallery, New York.

162 Alessandri, *La Ragazza di Amsterdam (The Girl from Amsterdam)*, 1966, oil, 200 x 122 cm. Courtesy J.-M. Lo Duca, Paris.

163 Alessandri, *La Ragazza del Ristorante Indochinese (The Girl of the Vietnamese Restaurant)*, 1966, oil, 200 x 122 cm. Courtesy J.-M. Lo Duca, Paris.

164 Roland Delcol, *Sans Paroles (Without Words)*, 1970, oil, 60 x 80 cm. Courtesy J.-M. Lo Duca, Paris; Galerie Isy Brachot, Brussels, Paris.

165 George Staempfli, *Sierra Blanca*, 1976, pencil and watercolor, 31.8 x 25.4 cm. Collection of Robert Van Roijen, Florida.

166 Mary Frank, *Lovers*, 1977, two part monoprint, 60.3 x 89.5 cm. Zabriskie Gallery, New York.

167 Frank, *Lovers*, 1975, ceramic, 22.8 x 11.4 x 8.3 cm. Zabriskie Gallery, New York.

168 Sassona Sakel, *A Yellow Night*, 1978, acrylic, 111.8 x 228.6 cm. Collection of W. Norton.

169 Robert Andrew Parker, untitled, 1979, watercolor, Terry Dinten-fass Gallery, New York.

170-171 Martin Hoffman, *Beggarman, Thief*, 1977, oil, 56 x 89 cm. Reproduced by special permission of PLAYBOY magazine, © 1977 by Playboy.

172-173 H.R. Giger, *Paysage XX, D'où venons-nous? (Landscape #20, Where are we coming from?)*, 1973, acrylic on paper, 100 x 70 cm. Collection Bijan Aalam, Paris.

174 Anthony Green, *Self Portrait with Our New Wallpaper*, 1974, oil on board, 213.4 x 129.5 cm. Collection of the artist; Rowan Gallery, London.

175 John DeAndrea, (left) *Jennifer*, cast vinyl polychromed in oil, lifesize. Collection of Mr. and Mrs. David Levin, Terre Haute, Indiana.

(right) DeAndrea, *Couple*, 1978, lifesize. Courtesy O.K. Harris Works of Art, New York; Photo by D. James Dee.

176-177 Andy Warhol, *Torso Series*, 1977, oil, 81.3 x 198.1 cm. Ace Gallery, Los Angeles.

178-179 Warhol, *Torso Series*, 1977, oil, 127 x 289.6 cm. Ace Gallery, Los Angeles.

Beyond Realism

181 Larry Rivers, *The Lamp Man Loves It*, 1966, mixed media with light, 269.2 x 165.1 cm. Collection of the artist, New York.

183 André Masson, *Dancer*, watercolor, 52.7 x 36.8 cm. Collection of Bradley Smith.

184-185 Masson, from *Mythologie Sexuelle* lithograph series, 1973, 137.2 x 193 cm. Collection of Bradley Smith.

187 Salvador Dali, *Vertige (Vertigo)*, 1932, oil, 60 x 51.5 cm. Galerie André-François Petit, Paris.

188-189 Max Ernst, *Le Jardin des Hespérides (The Garden of the Hesperides)*, 1935, oil, 81 x 100 cm. Galerie André-François Petit, Paris.

190-191 Roberto Matta Echaurren, *War of the Sexes*, colored pencil, 55.9 x 71.1 cm. Collection of Victor Lownes, London.

192 Paul Wunderlich, *Black Torso*, 1969, gouache, 88.9 x 71 cm. Collection of Philip A. Bruno, New York.

193 Sostras, untitled, 1973, Courtesy M. d'Halluin, Galerie 3 + 2, Paris.

195 Hans Bellmer, *Les Bas Rayés (Striped Stockings)*, lithograph after painting, 134 x 175 cm. Collection of Bradley Smith.

196-197 Bellmer, *Cephalopod With Portrait of Unica Zurn and Hans Bellmer*, 1955, painting, collage, 55 x 81 cm. Galerie André-François Petit, Paris.

198 Amaral, *Plante enracinée aux deux bouts (Plant rooted at both ends)*, 1977, mixed media, 30 x 21 cm. Galerie Negru, Paris.

199 Friedrich Schröder-Sonnenstern, *Die Praxis (The Practice)*, colored chalk, 51 x 73 cm. Courtesy M. d'Halluin, Galerie 3 + 2, Paris.

200-201 Gérard Deuquet, *Les Couples*, 1975, oil, 65 x 98 cm. Courtesy J.-M. Lo Duca, Paris.

202 Deuquet, *La Pomme d'Adam (The Apple of Adam)*, 1969, oil, 70 x 60 cm. Courtesy J.-M. Lo Duca, Paris; Private collection, Brussels.

203 Manfred Marburger, *Apple II*, 1977, acrylic, ink, colored pencil on wood, 76 x 76 cm. Aberbach Fine Art, London.

204-205 Stehli, *Nu sur une Table (Nude on a Table)*, oil, 90 x 130 cm. Musée du Petit Palais, Geneva.

206 Volker Stoecks, *Health and Strength II*, 1979, acrylic, 267 x 176 cm. Aberbach Fine Art, London.

207 Mihail Chemiakin, *Harlequin and Petruska*, 1978, gouache, 30.5 x 30.5 cm. Eduard Nakhamkin Fine Arts, Inc., New York.

208 Francisco Toledo, *La Ronda*, 1965, gouache, 39.4 x 45.1 cm. Collection of Harold Hart, New York.

209 Richard Lindner, *Le Couple*, 1961, oil, 94 x 63 cm. Galerie Claude Bernard, Paris.

210 Richard Oliver, untitled, oil, 127 x 86.4 cm. Collection of Jacques Kaplan, New York.

211 Igor Medvedev/Mead, *Bindu-Yoni*, 1972, mixed media, 101.6 x 76.2 cm. Collection of the artist, Palo Alto, California

212 George Segal, *Delta of Venus*, sculpture, collection of Paul Jenkins, New York.

Books by Bradley Smith

The American Way of Sex
Erotic Art of the Masters:
The 18th, 19th & 20th Centuries
The Emergency Book: You Can Save a Life
(with Gus Stevens)
The New Photography
The USA: A History in Art
China: A History in Art (with Wan-Go Weng)
Mexico: A History in Art
Spain: A History in Art
Japan: A History in Art
The Horse in the West
The Life Of The Giraffe
The Life Of The Elephant
The Life Of The Hippopotamus
Columbus in the New World
The Horse In The Blue Grass Country
Escape To The West Indies

Producer—Editor

Insomnia or The Devil At Large, by Henry Miller
My Life And Times, by Henry Miller
The Golden Sea, by Joseph E. Brown
Art For Children, by Ernest Raboff (15 titles)